The Quilt That Walked to Golden

SANDRA DALLAS

with Nanette Simonds

PHOTOGRAPHY BY POVY KENDAL ATCHISON

Breckling Press

Library of Congress Cataloging-in-Publication Data

Dallas, Sandra.

The quilt that walked to Golden : women and quilts of the Mountain
West : from the Overland Trail to contemporary Colorado / Sandra Dallas,
with Nanette Simonds ; photography by Povy Kendal Atchison.

p. cm.

Includes bibliographical references and index.

ISBN 10: 1-933308-17-6; ISBN 13: 978-1-9333081-7-3

1. Quiltmakers—West (U.S.)—Biography. 2. Women pioneers—West
(U.S.)—Biography. 3. Quilts—West (U.S.)—Themes, motives. 4. Quilting—
West (U.S.)—History—19th century. I. Simonds, Nanette. II. Title.

NK9197.D35 2004

746.46′092′278—dc22

2004015503

This book was set in Kepler by Bartko Design, Inc.
Editorial direction by Anne Knudsen
Cover and interior design by Kim Bartko, Bartko Design, Inc.
Author photograph and interior photography by Povy Kendal Atchison unless otherwise credited
Patterns by Cindy Sanders Harp
Technical editing and drawings by Kandy Petersen

Excerpt from "Magenta" on page 39 appears in *Westering* by Thomas Hornsby Ferril, © 1934 by Yale University Press.

Published by Breckling Press
283 Michigan St., Elmhurst, IL 60126

Released in paperback in 2007

Second printing. Printed and bound in China.

ISBN 10: 1-933308-17-6; ISBN 13: 978-1-9333081-7-3

*Opposite right, Nine Patch Doll Quilt, c. 1940, made by
Carrie Effa (Faye) McCauley Dallas, Harveyville, Kans.
Cottons, hand-pieced and hand-quilted, 19¾″ × 23″.
Faye, who was the model for Sabra Ritter in her grand-
daughter's novel,* The Persian Pickle Club, *made the quilt
for Donna Kay Dallas, the author's older sister.*

From Sandra to Faye Dallas

From Nanette to George, Susan,

Steven, and Amie

Contents

Acknowledgments

Just as many hearts and hands are necessary to make a friendship quilt, *The Quilt That Walked to Golden* would not have been possible without the contributions of so many people. Barbara Daubenspeck generously loaned us copies of her interviews with Eugenia Mitchell. They not only tell Eugenia's story, but capture her wit and humor. Eugenia's brother Ruben Hartmeister and daughter Mary Ellen Gray, along with Teri Dubois and Marie Overdier shared recollections of the Rocky Mountain Quilt Museum founder. Margaret Geick provided information on her great-grandmother Mary Jane Burgess and her family.

The Rocky Mountain Quilt Museum's former president Pat Moore and former director Janet Finley helped conceptualize the book. Assistant administrator Opal Frey spent hours checking facts and sharing her vast knowledge of quilts. We're indebted to Rudy Giecek, Ila Small Lingelbach, Connie Primus, and Alberta Iliff Shattuck for background information, and to historians Barbara Brackman, Clark Secrest, Ann Olsen, Nell Brown Propst, Mary Ann Schmidt, Wendy Ware, and Jeananne Wright.

Quilters are a sharing lot. Among those who shared their knowledge are Nancy Gelbhaus, Cindy Harp, Patty Hawkins, Pat Hubbard, Shirley Sanden, Robbie Spillman, David Taylor, Ricky Tims, and Judith Trager, as well as Nancy A. Jones and the Friendly Ladies of the Cloth, Opal Roderick and the Last Chance Quilters, Vi Cribbs and the Seven Sisters Quilt Guild, Toni Fitzwater and the Sisterhood of Purple, Gwinn Downton, Jessica Vaughn, Milinda Walker, and the members of the Rocky Mountain Wa Shonaji Quilt Guild. Thanks, too, to Marge Hedges, Bonnie Leman, Mary Leman Austin, Sandy Phillips, and Paulette Tilden.

We are indebted to Moya Hansen and Alisa Zahller at the Colorado Historical Society; Kelly Murphy at the Colorado Springs Pioneers Museum; Imelda DeGraw, Libbie Gottschalk, and Alice Zrebiec at the Denver Art Museum; the staff of the Western History Department, Denver Public Library; Elinor E. Packard at the Golden Pioneer Museum; Lorena Orvañanos Donohue at the Littleton Historical Museum; Lory Morrow at the Montana Historical Society; Sissi Williams at the Loyd Files Research Library, Museum of Western Colorado; Kathy Brougham at the Plains Conservation Center; and Pamela Laird at the University of Colorado, Denver. Cindy Harp provided the patterns.

Povy Kendal Atchison made the book come alive with her photographs. Dana Atchison, Cindy Brick, Nancy Riddle Iversen, Ron Penton, and Paulette Tilden shared their historical photos.

A special thanks to Auriel Orem Sandstead, Colorado's first lady of quilting.

And our gratitude to Danielle Egan-Miller of Browne & Miller Literary Associates and to Jane Jordan Browne, who got *The Quilt That Walked to Golden* started but did not live to see it completed. A final thanks to Anne Knudsen and Kim Bartko at Breckling Press for making this such a splendid book.

Prologue

The Quilt That Walked to Golden

In 1864, Mary Jane Paulson Burgess, about twenty-six, packed up her household belongings for the long trip across the prairie from Columbus, Ohio, to Golden City, Colorado Territory. Mary Jane's husband, Thomas W. Burgess, thirty-four, had recently returned from a trip west where he had prospected for gold. The precious metal was discovered in Colorado just six years earlier, and he had hoped to make his fortune there. But Thomas fell ill, and when he recovered, he concluded that he was not cut out for the manual labor of a prospector, working outdoors in the cold and rain. He looked for something more to his liking and discovered Golden.

Meadow Daisy, or Black-Eyed Susan, 1875–1900, maker unknown. Cottons, hand-pieced, hand-appliquéd, and hand-quilted, 84" × 84½".

The Quilt That Walked to Golden

Located at the edge of the mountains, Golden was a supply point for the mining towns farther west and was so important that from 1862 to 1867, it was Colorado's territorial capital. The Civil War had deprived the town of money for growth, however, and Burgess saw a prosperous outlook for a man who could provide Golden with necessities.[1] His future, as the saying went, was not in mining but in mining the miners.

So Burgess returned to Ohio, and he and Mary Jane and their daughter Alice, age two, along with Thomas's brother, Jacob, and his wife, another Mary, prepared for the trip west. Thomas purchased building materials to construct a business block and loaded them into a covered wagon (or perhaps, because two families were going west, there were two wagons). The conveyance was crowded with doors and windows, hammers, saws, and kegs of nails, leaving little room for necessities, let alone luxuries. As a space-saving measure, Mary Jane packed her china plates and cups in barrels of flour. The two women sold or gave away prized possessions that were too bulky to transport. Even then, there was no room in the wagon for trunks of clothes, and Thomas told the women that they could take along only the apparel that they could wear.

Unwilling to leave behind their clothes, the two Marys layered their dresses and skirts, blouses and petticoats. Bundled up in their entire wardrobes, they made the journey from Ohio to Golden, much of it by foot.[2] Like most pioneers who crossed the prairie in covered wagons, the Burgesses probably traveled ten to twenty miles a day, which meant a journey of perhaps three months. The trip would have been both arduous and monotonous for the women, who undoubtedly walked much of the way, their layers of skirts dragging in the dust, rather than ride on the hard wagon seat. As they walked along, they would have searched for wild greens to vary their diet of bacon and beans and soda biscuits. They probably picked up buffalo chips and put them into canvas bags. The Marys used the buffalo dung to fuel their campfires, since little wood was available. They cooked, bent over heavy iron pots suspended on tripods above the flames, while the wind drove smoke and powdered buffalo chips into their faces and clothes. There was always the danger that a spark would set a heavy skirt on fire.

If they observed the Sabbath, as many pioneers did, they did not rest but baked bread, and mended and washed clothes—that is, when water was available. Rarely did they have the opportunity to bathe. Mary Jane would have been responsible for little Alice, protecting her from wagon wheels and rattlesnakes, and, as a woman, she would have cared for anyone who was sick. Like their husbands, the women probably drove the wagons from time to time and kept watch for Indians, although illness and accidents were far more dangerous than the Native Americans. In those early years, most pioneers traveled in companies for protection. Mary Jane would have enjoyed the society of other women but hated the dirt thrown up by dozens of pairs of oxen. When they felt safe, the two Marys probably walked a little distance away from the wagon dust, perhaps picking wildflowers and dreaming about what life held for them in Colorado Territory.

Thomas built his hotel at 1015 Ford Street, in what became the Goosetown section of Golden, so-named because geese were raised there. Completed in 1866, the Burgess Block opened as saloon, store, and public hall where early-day balls and political gatherings were held. In 1872, the building was remodeled and renamed the Burgess House, a hotel and dining hall, known for good food. Indeed, in 1881, the Burgess House advertised that its chef had once worked at Charpiot's Restaurant, Denver's finest eatery.

The Quilt That Walked to Golden or Lone Star, date unknown. Cottons, hand-pieced and hand-quilted, 76½" × 77¾". Known in the family as the quilt that Mary Jane Burgess made from the clothes she wore as she walked from Ohio to Golden in 1864, this quilt actually is constructed from later fabrics. Most likely, it is a copy of Mary Jane's quilt and may have been made by her granddaughter, Marion Burgess Geick.

Burgess House prices were reasonable, with dinner at thirty-five cents. Just what that included is not known, but if the meal was typical, it was heavy on meat, potatoes, and root vegetables, with pie for dessert. Although they kept a connection with the hotel—for a time, Mary Jane was listed as proprietor—the family later was involved in ranching and the express business. Two sons became druggists at the Windsor Hotel in Denver.

In the 1860s, an era that offered scant leisure in the Colorado towns, Mary Jane kept busy in her new home, and if she had spare time, she sewed. As the red and blue calico dresses she had worn on the overland trek wore out, she ripped them up and put the pieces aside for quilts. Later, she used the cotton fabric from her pioneer wardrobe to piece a Lone Star quilt top. Perhaps she picked the pattern because it reminded her of starry nights on the Great Plains, or maybe she selected it because stars were the most popular 19th century quilt patterns. The top most likely was quilted after Mary Jane's death, possibly by her granddaughter, Marion Burgess Geick. The family dubbed the bedcover The Quilt That Walked to Golden.

There is disappointingly little information available on Mary Jane Burgess. The tale of the quilt came from her granddaughter, Marion, who gave both the story and the quilt to the Rocky Mountain Quilt Museum in 1991, not long before she died. She never told her children about the quilt. Nor did she elaborate on Mary Jane's trip west. Did Mary Jane and her sister-in-law travel with other female relatives or women friends who also wore their clothes in layers? And did Mary Jane's daughter, Alice, scurry along the Overland Trail in dress upon dress? What happened to the second Mary and her husband, Jacob? They are not listed as Golden residents in the 1870 Colorado census, so they must have moved on. Like the quilts themselves, the stories of their pioneer makers are made up of fragments.

Westering

"5 quilts was none to(o) much cover."

Sarah Sutton

Green Russell, a Georgian with a braided beard and a party of sixty men, discovered gold just east of the Rocky Mountains in 1858, on a site soon to become Denver. Using large pie-shaped gold pans, the men panned less than $1,000 worth of gold from the waters of the Cherry Creek and the South Platte River that summer, but no matter. The word got out, and the Pikes Peak gold rush was on. The famed mountain was seventy-five miles south of Denver, but it nonetheless gave its name to the stampede of men to the Cherry Creek Diggings. Within months of the Russell discovery, newcomers had filled the nascent town with log houses and stores, saloons and gambling halls, carpentry and wagon-making shops. There were even a funeral home and a cemetery called Jack O'Neil's Ranch, later Cheesman Park.

LeMoyne Star, 1889, made by M.K. Smith. Cottons, hand-pieced and hand-quilted, 72″ × 75½″.

The Quilt That Walked to Golden

"Going To Be Rich, All Round"

That fall, Count Henri Murat, as he called himself, a self-proclaimed descendent of Joachim Murat, King of Naples under Napoleon, arrived with his wife, Katrina. He wrote to a friend that the journey across the prairie had been "a pleasure trip. My wife is well and getting fat. She looks as blooming and fresh as a maiden"—a generous description of the plump, potato-faced Katrina. The Murats opened the diggings' first hotel, the Eldorado, a hewn-log, one-story structure with a squat tower on top. Katrina tore up her petticoat to make a flag that the Count flew from the tower. Apart from mending done by the prospectors, Katrina's flag may have been the first serious sewing done in Colorado.[1]

Thousands of Americans were feverish to join the rush to the Rockies before the gold had all been discovered. And as many as nineteen guidebooks advised the would-be millionaires on necessities to pack and routes to take. Many of the guidebook authors either had not been west or knew nothing about finding gold. One suggested taking along a wooden boat with iron rasps on the bottom. The gold seeker could hoist the contraption to the top of Pikes Peak, then ride it to the bottom. The rasps would scrape off shavings of gold, as much as a ton per trip.[2] Most prospectors did not expect boatloads of gold, but more than one packed a wheelbarrow to pick up the gold nuggets he expected to find.

Guide to the Gold Mines of Kansas (Colorado was part of Kansas Territory when the Pikes Peak gold rush started) summed up the excitement: "Ho! For gold! We're a'goin'! Wagons making. Clothes preparing. Our business abandoning. Selling our houses. Putting off our wives and children upon their relations, or leaving them alone by themselves. Going to be rich, all round. No use being poor. No use to plod along, for your mere living, with your nose and belly in the dust, and your heels in the air. Oh no! Here we go for Pike's Peak. Times are hard—we go to Pike's Peak. Will be better no doubt, at Pike's Peak. So say many of our city people, and away goes their prosperity, their homes and firesides, and happy prospective of their families, and their own personal comforts."[3]

And They Sewed

Despite their anxiousness to "go for Pike's Peak," the pioneers spent months or up to a year preparing for the trip west. Men saw to the wagons and animals, weapons, farm equipment, and gold prospecting tools. Whether their destination was Colorado or far-

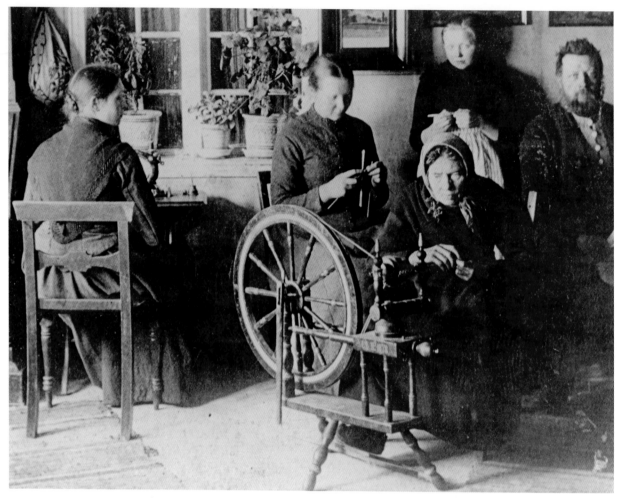

Before embarking on the westward journey, women spent months spinning and weaving, crocheting, knitting, and stitching.

ther west to California or Oregon, the women salted meats and dried fruit and sweet corn, purchased coffee, rice, and beans, and barrels of sugar and flour. They packed dishes, clothing, utensils, needles and thread, and sometimes even sewing machines. And they sewed.

There was hardly a woman of the time who did not know how to use a needle. Sewing was a critical household skill in an era when women were required to make most if not all of their family's clothing and bedding. "There is no accomplishment of any kind more desirable for a woman, than neatness and skill in the use of a needle.

To some, it is an employment not only useful, but absolutely necessary; and it furnishes a tasteful amusement to all," wrote Mrs. L. Maria Child in *The Girls' Own Book*, an 1834 tome designed to teach young girls to be useful.

Amusement was hardly the chief end of sewing, in Mrs. Child's view. Keeping little hands busy and training girls in women's skills were more important. "Little girls often have a great many small bits of cloth, and large remnants of time, which they don't know what to do with; and I think it is better for them to make cradle-quilts for their dolls, or their baby brothers, than to be standing around, wishing they had something to do. The pieces are arranged in a great variety of forms: squares, diamonds, stars, blocks, octagon pieces placed in circles, &c. A little girl should

Needlework was a lifetime occupation. Girls learned to sew and knit before they could write, and stitched until their eyes were dim.

examine whatever kind she wishes to imitate, and cut a paper pattern, with great care and exactness," Mrs. Child wrote.[4]

"Children can very early be taught to . . . knit garters, suspenders, and stockings; they can make patchwork and braid straw," Mrs. Child continued in a second book, *The American Frugal Housewife*, probably the best-known of all the advice books written for women in the first half of the 1800s. She noted that "patchwork is good economy. It is indeed a foolish waste of time to tear cloth into bits for the sake of arranging it anew in fantastic figures; but a large family may be kept out of idleness, and a few shillings saved, by thus using scraps of gowns, curtains, &c."[5]

Wool from home-grown sheep was made into cloth or was sometimes used as batting in quilts.

Idleness was to be greatly feared. A girl who was not serious about learning the worthwhile craft of sewing was a pitiful creature in nineteenth-century children's literature. In *Good Little Girls' Book*, which, like most children's books of the time was written to instruct as well as entertain, editor Mrs. Sarah Jane Hale wrote despairingly of seven-year-old Fanny Tribe, "one of the giddiest little things in the world . . . when the hour for sitting down to work arrives, you may always hear Fanny making such enquiries as these: 'Oh, Kate, have you seen my thimble?' 'Do you know where my needle-case is, Betsey?' 'Dear me! I cannot find my scissors; can any body tell me where they are?'"

Was there hope for such a foolish little girl? Only if Fanny learned to emulate her cheerful, if docile, older sister, Ellen, or if she were punished by, say, having to spend her own pocket money to purchase the misplaced item. "I dare say, if they reflect on the subject, they will find that they are seldom guilty of carelessness without having cause to be sorry for it afterwards," observed Mrs. Hale.[6]

Teaching naughty little Fanny Tribe her place was the duty of a well-to-do mother. Most little girls in those days rarely had their own thimbles and scissors, and certainly, they did not have pocket money to purchase them. In mid-nineteenth-century America, many mothers didn't have the money for store-bought cloth, either. Before these women could cut and sew, they first had to manufacture the fabric. Families raised sheep for wool, which was carded and spun at home. They grew flax that through a complicated and time-consuming process was turned into homespun linen cloth.

Girls learned domestic skills at an early age. "For my thirteenth birthday I was given a spinning wheel," wrote Kate Morris, an Oregon immigrant.[7]

If the women wanted their clothes to be anything but white or a natural color, they home-dyed the cloth, using purchased compounds or dyes made from wild plants. And dyeing was no easy matter. Dr. A.W. Chase, the nineteenth century author of a dozen household medical guides that advised women on everything from how to make a vinegar pie to how to cure venereal disease, detailed dyeing methods. To dye lengths of cotton or linen blue by using logwood, he wrote, "In all cases, if new, they should be boiled in strong soap suds or weak-lye and rinsed clean; then for cotton 5 lbs. or linen 3 lbs., take bi-chromate of potash ¾ lb.; put in the goods and dip 2 hours, then take out, rinse; make a dye with logwood 4 lbs.; dip in this 1 hour, air and let stand in the dye 3 or 4 hours, or till the dye is almost cold, wash out and dry."[8]

Once the fabric was ready, homemakers cut out clothes and stitched them by hand, since few women had access to sewing machines until long after the Civil War. Precious scraps were salvaged and used for trim, or they were carefully saved in ragbags for piecework.

A sewing machine saved hours of labor, but any woman with such a magical appliance was probably wealthy.

Before they left for Colorado, "Mother ... got cotton and wool which she carded, then spun; dyed and wove yard after yard of sheets, bed spreads, dress goods and even 'jeans' for men's pants. My mother also took all of the old clothing and made it into rag carpets," recalled Georgia L. McRoberts, whose family moved from Mississippi to a homestead in Colorado's South Platte Valley in 1876.[9]

"Quilts Don't Answer Very Well on the Road"

Georgia's family's preparations were little different from those a generation earlier when Catherine Scott Coburn and her family had readied themselves for the trek west from her home near Pekin, Illinois: "Through all the winter preceding the April morning when the final start was made, the fingers of the women and girls were busy providing additional stores of bedding and blankets, of stockings and sunbonnets, of hickory shirts and gingham aprons, that the family might be equipped for the trip, and not left destitute in case of failure to reach the goal in season, or of opportunity to replenish the stores from the meager and high-priced stocks of a new country. Ah! the tears that fell upon these garments, fashioned with trembling fingers by the flaring light of tallow candles; the heartaches that were stitched and knitted and woven into them, through the brief winter afternoons, as relatives that were to be left behind and friends of a lifetime dropped in to lend a hand in the awesome undertaking of getting ready for a journey that promised no return. . . ."

Once the preparations were done, Catherine continued, "The wagon bed was packed with boxes and bundles neatly stored; a feather bed and pillows, rolled together and tied with cord during the day, were at night made up for a couch, with quilts and blankets, in a space made vacant by the removal of the boxes."[10]

Since the guidebooks plagiarized each other, they gave much the same recommendations on provisions and equipment to take west. One book advised men to take with them a tent and poles, ten pairs of blankets (at $4 per pair), but "leave your razor, for you won't use it."[11] Another suggested that "A pair of stout Mackinaw blankets, blue or gray, should be carried." The author also recommended packing them in a trunk that was "of moderate size, and of the strongest make. Test it by throwing it from the top of a three-storied house; if you pick it up uninjured, it will do to go to Kansas. Not otherwise."[12]

Yet another author wrote, "Plenty of bed-clothing should not be neglected, among which should also be an empty tick, which can be filled, after you stop, for use."[13] While many guidebook authors had never even seen the Shining Mountains, as the Colorado Rockies were called, they figured the mining camps would be cold and recommended ten blankets per traveler. Blankets were preferred over quilts. A Minnesota man who went to Montana in search of gold wrote his wife in 1863, "Quilts don't answer very well on the road. They get torn too easy."[14]

Men traveling overland preferred blankets, but women refused to leave their precious quilts behind. This woman was the model for the title character in the novel, Alice's Tulips, *set during the Civil War.*

Carolina Lily variation, c. 1850–1900, made by Amelia Flavia Russell Tilden, Pennsylvania. Cotton, hand-pieced and hand-quilted, 83″ × 86″. A 1931 article about Amelia's 102 birthday reported that Amelia never lived more than a few miles from Watrous Corners, Penn., where she was born in 1829. She died in 1932.

Such advice may have kept solitary men in blankets, but it probably didn't dissuade women from taking along their cherished quilts, no matter how impractical or heavy. And quilts could be quite heavy, as Julia Archibald Holmes, an adventurer who became the first white woman to climb 14,110-foot Pikes Peak, discovered. In her book *A Bloomer Girl on Pike's Peak 1858*, she wrote, "My own pack weighed 17 pounds; nine of which were bread, the remainder a quilt and clothing. James' pack weighed 35 pounds." Among the things that James Holmes, Julia's husband, toted up the mountain were ten pounds of bread, one pound of hog meat, eating utensils, a half-gallon canteen, a book of Ralph Waldo Emerson's essays, and five quilts.[15]

Some women undoubtedly made quilts specifically for the journey west, that is, if they had time left over after stitching clothing and even tents. Mary Hayden, who crossed the plains and Rocky Mountains on her way to Oregon in 1850, wrote, "We had to have a new tent as ours was too small and my husband was going to buy one, but they had none that I liked. In looking over the camp I found one that just suited me, but could not get one made like it as they had no pattern. I said that I could make one, but was ridiculed for the idea, but finally Mr. Hayden got the ozenberg [osnaburg] and in two weeks we had a tent that I was very proud of. It had laped seams too. I was greatly complimented for one so young, for I was not quite out of my teens yet. Mr. Copeland helped me to measure and sew the tent as I had planned and cut it."[16]

Augusta Tabor, whose husband, Horace, was to become Colorado's first silver king, arrived in Colorado in 1859. While her husband and a travelling companion headed for the Gregory Diggings, later Central City, the weary Augusta stayed behind near Golden with her sick child "in the 7 × 9 tent, that my hands had made."[17] For years, Augusta loyally followed her husband from camp to camp, living in a tent or a log cabin, operating a post office, store, and boarding house for the miners, while her husband prospected for gold or sat near the stove, gossiping with prospectors. Tabor was a soft touch and often grubstaked miners, providing food and supplies in exchange for one-third of any mineral the prospectors found. In 1878, two prospectors Tabor had grubstaked hit pay dirt with the discovery of the silver-rich Little Pittsburg mine near Leadville.

In the next few years, the Tabors became fabulously wealthy, but their marriage did not survive, and Tabor left Augusta for a younger woman, Elizabeth McCourt Doe, known as Baby Doe. Tabor lost much of his fortune in the 1893 silver crash and the rest through bad investments in mines and natural resources. He died penniless in 1899, and Baby Doe moved to a mine shack outside Leadville, where she froze to death in 1935. By then, Augusta was long dead, leaving behind a tidy fortune that she had made herself by investing her divorce settlement.[18]

If they didn't make tents, many women fashioned wagon sheets, or covers, for their prairie schooners, some even growing flax, processing it into linen thread, then weaving the fabric for the wagon top. Keturah Belknap spun thread to be made into fabric for a wagon cover for her 1848 trip from Iowa. "Will spin mostly evenings while my husband reads to me. The little wheel in the corner don't make any noise. I spin for Mother B. and Mrs. Hawley and they will weave; now that it is in the loom I must work almost day and night to get the filling ready to keep the loom busy."[19] There also was the business of making mattress ticks and filling them with grass or straw or feathers. "We have 30 tame geese to pick . . . we will pick them once more and then sell them . . . we shall take with us 6 feather beds," wrote Sarah Sutton, who was bound for Oregon in 1854. Family legend says Sarah also stitched a shroud for an ailing daughter who was not expected to complete the trip. The daughter did not need the shroud, but Sarah did. She died on the Overland Trail.[20]

Pickle Dish, c. 1880, maker unknown. Cottons, hand-pieced and hand-quilted, 65" × 73".

AHAHE

WICHITA

No 1117

On the Overland Trail

Sarah Sutton may have been optimistic with her six ticks. Wagon beds were small and could accommodate only part of what the pioneers wanted to take with them—as Mary Jane Burgess had discovered when she donned all her clothing for the trip to Golden. Moreover, what did make it into the wagon had to be meticulously organized. Keturah Belknap wrote that the first thing she and her husband, George, loaded into their wagon bed was a big box containing bacon, salt, and other foodstuffs. The box's wooden cover did double duty as a table. The Belknaps added a clothes chest and a medicine chest, a chest for dishes that would not be unpacked until they reached their destination, a chair, and five home-made linen sacks, each filled with 125 pounds of flour or cornmeal. Along one wall were stacked sacks of dried apples and peaches, beans, rice, sugar, and green coffee. Then there were the earthenware and ironware dishes to be used on the trip, cooking pots and utensils, and a few toys for the Belknaps' son, Jessie. All that left no room for a bed, so Keturah expected to "level up the sacks with some extra bedding . . . then two comforts and we have a good enough bed for anyone to sleep on." The sensible Keturah also "cut out some sewing to have to pick up at all the odd moments" crossing the country.[21]

There were few such odd moments on the Overland Trail, for the women worked alongside their men, driving the wagons and herding cattle. During noonings and at the end of the day, women prepared meals, usually over campfires, since few pioneers took along stoves. At night, they cooked, washed clothing, and tended their children, along with any sick or dying. Only when those chores were done, did they sew, and then it usually was mending.

"Mrs. Wilson made a spinning wheel out of a grindstone they had with them. When they stopped to rest, she spun woolen yarn and knit it into socks and stockings as they rode along," Orpha Baldwin McNitt wrote home to her family in Wisconsin in 1870. Orpha had just immigrated to Evans, Colorado.[22]

"Cool and pleasant; saw the first Indians today. Lucy and Almira afraid and run into the wagon to hide. Done some washing and sewing," Amelia Stewart Knight wrote in her overland journal on April 29, 1853.[23] Another time, Amelia noted that she had "been sewing and cooking to day, the mosquitoes are very bad here. . . ." The next day, she was still at it: "Still in camp, overhauling the wagons, cooking sewing

Native Americans, such as this Wichita woman,
learned quilting techniques from white women. Some
travelers traded needles and thread to the Indians, and
a few mended the Indians' clothes.

Chestnut Burr or Pineapple, c. 1890 top made by "Grandmother" Bedell and her daughters Fannie, Mary, Margaret, and Arminda, Pennsylvania. Cottons, foundation-pieced by machine, 64⅞" × 65⅛". Backing may be grain or feed sacks.

The Quilt That Walked to Golden

patching. . . ."[24] A year later, Elizabeth Myrick, heading for California, wrote: "Some are patching an[d] mending their clothes I have been sewing the waggon sheets. . . ."[25] The only respite seemed to come with bad weather. "It has been too cold for sewing and the road has been so rough and uneven that I accomplished but little with the needle," Helen Carpenter recorded in her journal on July 3, 1857. Helen, who had just left Fort Riley, Kansas, apparently was trying to stitch while riding in a covered wagon.[26]

Little girls, too, were enlisted in the endless job of mending clothes. "My three daughters are around me one at my side trying to sew," wrote Tamsen E. Donner to her sister on May 11, 1846. Tamsen was resting in a tent in Independence, Missouri, on the way from her home in Springfield, Illinois, to California. She never finished the journey, of course. Tamsen's husband, George, was head of the ill-fated Donner party, whose members turned to cannibalism, eating their companions after they died, when they were stranded in blizzards in the Sierra mountains. Both Tamsen and her husband died in the snow, although all of their daughters survived.[27]

The quilts they brought with them undoubtedly were a comfort to women who had traded the security of home, family, and friends for the uncertainty of traveling through the vast prairies and treacherous mountains. The home-made quilts and comforts brought back memories of sitting by the hearth on quiet evenings, work baskets by their sides, as they cut shapes from worn gowns and baby dresses and stitched them into quilt pieces. They remembered being surrounded by friends, as they gossiped about a quilting frame. Many women brought along friendship quilts. Family and friends signed their names on quilt squares made in the Churn Dash or Chimney Sweep patterns. The squares

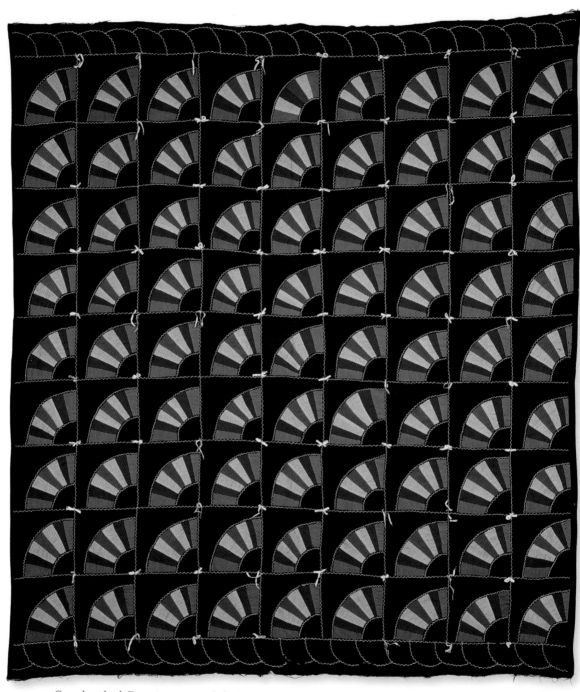

Grandmother's Fan, 1897, top made by Mrs. S.R. Sherwin, Harvard, Neb. Wool, hand-pieced, hand-embroidered, and hand-tied, 69½" × 76".

were assembled into a top that was quilted, often in secret, then presented to the woman as a going away present. The sight of a friendship quilt, tucked into a corner of a wagon was enough to bring any pioneer woman to tears.

Still, quilts were taken west not as sentimental objects but to be used. They served as bedding, of course. "5 quilts was none to[o] much cover, and it has not got warm yet at noon," wrote Sarah Sutton, the woman who had made a half-dozen feather beds for the journey.[28] Quilts were used as coats or shawls. "I bundle up in a comforter, as many others have to do, and as there's no one here whom I know or care for, my appearance gives me little concern," admitted Lucy Rutledge Cooke, who crossed the prairie in 1852.[29]

Quilts also served sobering purposes on the trek west, put to use as shrouds or protective covering. When her wagon train was attacked by Indians in 1862, Jane Gould "put up a mattress and some beds and quilts on the exposed side of the wagon to protect us." The wagon train was made up of one hundred and eleven wagons and two hundred men, and the damage was limited to a few bullet holes in the wagon sheets. But the pioneers were vigilant, and the next night, "We hung up a cotton mattress and some quilts and slept in the wagon."[30] A Kansas woman remembered the wagonmaster fastening quilts to the tops of covered wagons to keep out the rain.[31]

In a pinch, bedding was traded or sold. In Idaho, a pioneer woman observed that "One of our party sold a featherbed for $1.00 per lb . . . his wife refused for awhile to give up her feather bed but they must have something to eat and money to pay ferriage, so the feather bed went."[32] Another woman noted, "Sold our old feather bed for a sack of flower."[33]

Sewing items were a popular medium of exchange, especially with the Indians. "You mite trade a good deal with the Indians if you well take Blue Calico and Beeds in little narrow Red Blue & Green Ribbon" on the "Oragon" route, James M. Maxey, who already had gone west, advised James Frazier Reed in a letter written in 1845. Reed could also trade "Brown or Blch Muslins or Calico of any thing of that kind for common Bacon" at the forts he passed. But if Reed chose the "Sante Fee" route, "the goods you take must be blch & Bron Muslins and Calico of high colars very distect" for sale to the Spanish women.[34] Reed went the northern route, to his everlasting horror. He was one of the organizers of the Donner party, although he was luckier than Tamsen Donner: He survived.

Death

A grieving mother placed her beloved dead baby on the family's best quilt to be memorialized. The picture might be the only photograph ever taken of the child.

As women stitched quilts for the overland trip, they dreamed of life in their new homes in the West. Death was a part of that western life, however, so the quilts that brought comfort to the body on the Overland Trail sometimes brought solace to the soul at trail's end.

Catherine Haun, who traveled west in 1849, wrote of deaths "in this weird, lonely spot on God's footstool away apparently from everywhere and everybody. The bodies were wrapped together in a bed comforter and wound, quite mummified with a few yards of string that we made by tying together torn strips of a cotton dress skirt."[i]

Some pioneer women who had made quilts to adorn their Colorado homes used the bedcovers instead as winding sheets, as they left loved ones behind in lonely graves spaded into the prairie. Perhaps it brought a degree of comfort to a woman to know that a child or a husband or even a parent, for multi-generational families went west, rested forever in a quilt made by loving hands.

The trek west was a dangerous one. There was always the fear of Indians, of course, although Indians killed relatively few pioneers.

Far more deadly were dysentery, cholera, scurvy, and mountain fever, along with accidents, primarily drownings and gunshot wounds. Women died in childbirth and were burned when campfire sparks ignited their clothes. Children wandered off, were bitten by rattlesnakes, or crushed under wagon wheels. Men were trampled by oxen and even buffalo, and sometimes they were murdered. There are no figures for deaths among Colorado immigrants, but estimates are that perhaps six percent of the 350,000 pioneers who traveled overland between 1841 and 1866, whether to Colorado or farther west to Oregon and California, died in route. Legend says there are five graves for each mile of the 4,000-mile Oregon Trail.[ii]

Once they reached Colorado—or wherever their destination—pioneers found their new lives also were fraught with peril. Those who settled on farms died in accidents, were attacked by wild animals, or caught in ground blizzards; a man could become lost in a howling whiteness of the swirling snow and die only yards from the door of his house. Mining areas were even more treacherous. Men froze to death in the high mountains or were set on by footpads in the raw towns. They died by the score in avalanches and mine cave-ins.

"I think about my mother. In that window she would set, that window over there," wrote Breckenridge author Belle Turnbull in *The Far Side of the Hill,* which is set in a Colorado mining town. "Day after day she set there patching, when her housework would be done. Patching, darning, sewing for us kids, keeping an eye out in case a stretcher come down the trail. All day long she would keep the bed covers turned down, just in case."[iii] If the men with the stretcher turned in at her shack, the wife sat by her husband's bedside in the days ahead, patching, mending, as her husband himself mended. Or if he did not, his wife, her hands busy with sewing or quilting, kept a death watch.

The saddest deaths of all were those of the children, who were defenseless against childhood epidemics and the pneumonia that took so many of them at high altitudes. Family plots in early cemeteries often contain the graves of several children—a little girl who lived a year, her brother, age two, their stillborn sister, and then the mother, dead in childbirth. Sometimes, a beloved child, her little body calm in death, was laid out on the family's best quilt and a photographer called in to take the only picture ever made of her.

Sewing was a part of death, just as it was of life. A woman in Meeker, a Colorado ranching community, was employed to sew shrouds—and brought home the scraps for her daughter's doll clothes.[iv] When her sister died in childbirth, Grace Snyder, a pioneer Nebraska woman and well-known quilter, discovered pieces for a Wild Goose Chase quilt that the sister had cut out and stored in neat piles. Grace brought them home to turn them into a quilt for the infant. Grace herself gave birth to a stillborn child, blaming herself for the death, for she had spent hours at a treadle sewing machine. While her husband made a coffin, Grace wrapped the tiny infant for burial in a doll's quilt, to sleep for eternity in a pretty bit of feather-stitched silk.[v]

[i] Susan G. Butruille, *Women's Voices from the Oregon Trail: The Times That Tried Women's Souls and A Guide to Women's History Along the Oregon Trail,* (Boise: Tamarack Books Inc., 1993,) 100.
[ii] Merrill J. Mattes, *The Great Platte River Road,* (Lincoln: Nebraska State Historical Society, 1969,) 23. John D. Unruh, Jr., *The Plains Across: the Overland Emigrants and the Trans-Mississippi West, 1840–60,* (Urbana: University of Illinois Press, 1979,) 516.
[iii] Belle Turnbull, *The Far Side of the Hill,* (New York: Crown, 1953,) 37.
[iv] Julie Jones-Eddy, *Homesteading Women: An Oral History of Colorado 1890–1950,* (New York: Twayne Publishers, 1992,) 73.
[v] Grace Snyder as told to Nellie Snyder Yost, *No Time on My Hands,* (Caldwell: Caxton Printers Ltd., 1963, Reprint: Lincoln: University of Nebraska Press, 1986,) 335, 376–77.

Coralee's Quilt, c. 1900–1925, maker unknown. Wool, hand-pieced, hand-embroidered, and hand-quilted, 70½″ × 76½″. This mourning quilt, embroidered with chain-stitched hearts, plants, and other designs, memorializes Coralee Walters, born in 1885, died in 1894.

"Camped on the Snake, Indians came with salmon to sell. I let them have Helen's apron with a needle and thread and bought salmon enough for several meals," Lucia Loraine Williams wrote to her mother in 1851, after she arrived in Oregon.[35] "I had brought a supply of needles and thread, some of which I gave" to Sioux women, wrote Margaret A. Frink, in 1850.[36] The resourceful Sarah Sutton even sewed for the Indians: "here was two indians had on pants, some emegrant had give them, with their knees all out . . . they stood by me looking at me sew, and they haul'd of their pants and threw them down to me, and shewed me how they wanted them mended . . . according to orders I pached both pair, and they come up close to me and put them on well pleased."[37] Lorena L. Hays, stopping in Kansas in 1853 on her way to California, met some Kaw Indians, fed them breakfast, then obliged an Indian woman, who "begged some needles & thread."[38]

More often, it was white women who begged for thread and other sewing supplies, since such items were hard to come by in the remote West. Martha Missouri Moore was fortunate to find yard goods for just 20 cents a yard at Kearney, Nebraska, in 1860,[39] because farther west, fabric was difficult to find and expensive. Sarah Ann Milner Smith paid a dollar per yard for piece goods in 1864 in Central City. She noted that scarcity had driven up the price of other items, as well. "Wages barely kept even with expenses," she wrote. "Flour and potatoes were commonly twenty-five dollars per hundred weight, sugar and butter a dollar per pound, eggs fifteen cents apiece . . . freighting grew steadily more costly. Once when we were out of flour I saw my father stand for hours beside the road and wave a fifty dollar bill in the face of each teamster as he passed with loaded wagon in a futile attempt to purchase a sack."[40] Some gave up altogether trying to buy necessities and wrote home, asking that such items be

Unknown design, c. 1875, maker unknown. Cottons, hand- and machine-pieced, hand-appliquéd, and hand-quilted, 72" × 79".

The Quilt That Walked to Golden

sent, although it could take a year from the time the letter was mailed until the requested items were received. Mary Edgerton, a Montana pioneer, instructed her sister: " . . . black spool thread—coarse such as I shall want to use making pants for the boys. Send a number of spools of black and of the browns from number 30 to 40."[41] Tabitha Brown found a six-and-one-fourth cent piece (one-half of a "bit") in Salem, Oregon, in 1846 and spent it on three needles.[42]

Parting Gifts

Westering was considerably easier a generation later, when Mary Hallock Foote, a young bride, traveled to New Almaden, California, in 1876, to join her husband, Arthur, a mining engineer. Foote, who was to become the 19th century's best-known woman writer-illustrator of the American West, published sixteen books, including *The Led-Horse Claim: A Romance of a Mining Camp*, set in Leadville, Colorado. She lived in a log cabin in Leadville in 1879, where she worked on illustrations for national magazines such as *Scribner's Monthly* and *The Atlantic Monthly* and was the hostess of a sort of frontier literary salon.

On her initial journey west, Mary, loaded down with trunks and boxes, boarded the Overland Limited in Poughkeepsie, New York. Family and friends gave her so many parting gifts that Mary accused one generous woman of having "gone clean daft on the subject." Among the gifts was a silk quilt made by Mary's sister and a cousin. In the lonely years ahead, Mary, like thousands of other westering women, must have run her hands over the tiny stitches and thought nostalgically of the life she had left behind to find a home in the West.[43]

Settling In

"A quilt was sewed together . . . and passed on with love."

Pat Hubbard on her great-grandmother,
Emily Wilson

For Mollie Dorsey Sanford and other middle-class Victorian women, sewing was a necessary skill—just like cooking, scrubbing floors, and killing and plucking chickens. Mollie was more fortunate than many women of her time. She was good enough to earn a living with her needle. Not long after she and her family moved to Nebraska Territory in 1857, Mollie took a job as a seamstress. "I am now domiciled at Mrs. Burnham's and enjoying my feeling of independence. She is very fond of me and I could not be treated more considerately," Mollie wrote in her journal on May 6, 1858.

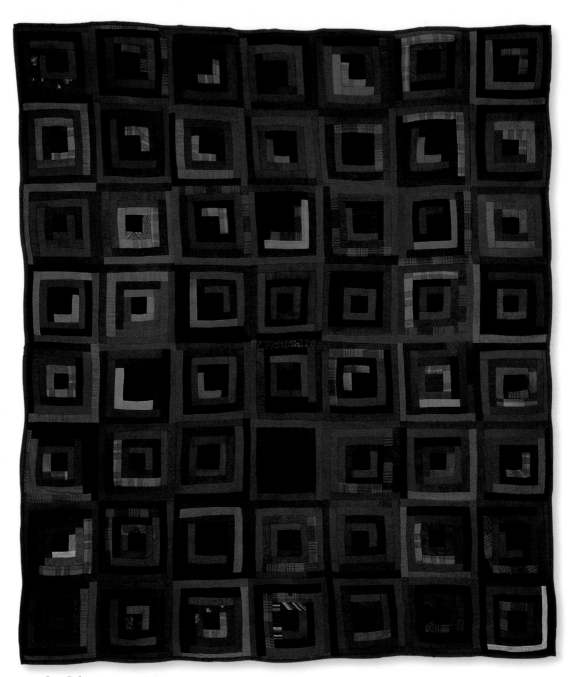

Log Cabin, 1890, made by Carrie Digerness Melum, Ellsworth, Iowa. Wools and velvets, machine-pieced and hand-quilted, 63½″ × 73½″.

The Quilt That Walked to Golden

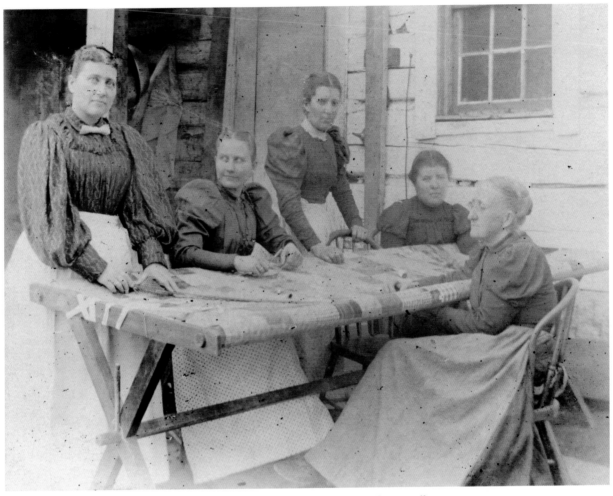

Pioneer women were never idle, and whenever they gathered, they took along their needles.

Still, there was a problem. Mrs. Burnham was "a woman of the world, however, and very much afraid I may not be taken into society if I am known to be working for her, so she says, 'Let them think you are visiting.' But no! I said, 'My dear, I sail under no false colors. I am henceforth to the public 'Mollie E. Dorsey, dressmaker and seamstress.' ' As such I now am, and getting along splendidly. Thanks to a mother's training, I am quite an adept at dressmaking."[1]

Women who did plain sewing were in great demand in gold and silver camps, although miners might have been reluctant to patronize this Ironton establishment.

And thanks to Mollie's own honesty and high spirits, being a seamstress had no negative effects on her social life. Less than two years later, on February 14, 1860, Mollie married Byron N. Sanford, and two months after that, the newlyweds left Nebraska for the Colorado gold camps.

As one of the few women in the mining towns—most of them established only weeks or months before she arrived—Mollie found her sewing skills in great demand. "I have traded sewing for a fine brahma rooster," she wrote on July 23. "I get fabulous prices for sewing."[2]

Sewing became a lifelong activity for Mollie. She and By Sanford eventually settled on a farm near Littleton, Colorado, and she continued to sew, as she raised children and worked the farm. On March 25, 1897, she wrote, "I attended the ladies aid. Two weeks from to day they meet here to do some quilting." Two weeks later, on April 6, she was preparing for the quilting bee. "I was busy all day arranging a room to put the quilt in the frame. This afternoon Mrs. Hicks and Mrs. Bell came over to [help], so to have all ready for the ladies." The event was a success, because the following day, she wrote, "The sun came out warm. By 10 o'clock the snow had melted, and ladies began to arrive. By noon there were 20. Some of the gents came to dinner. The quilt was finished, and all declared they never had a more pleasant social."

Mollie noted in one of her 1897 diary entries that she had not been "very 'spry' today. Worked on my quilt a while—read some, and so the day has passed."[3] And so, we can presume, her life passed. She continued to stitch until her death on February 6, 1915, at the age of seventy-six.[4]

"Every Decent Scrap of Cloth"

Since there were few places to purchase bedding, most pioneer families brought along enough to last at least through the first winter. "Every decent scrap of cloth was kept for quilt blocks. All women old and young, were supposed to help piece quilts. In the late 1800's, a girl of four had her stint of sewing quilt blocks before she could play," wrote Hazel Denney in her recollections of life in Veteran, Wyoming, *Veteran, District 13: Homesteading in Goshen Hole.*[5] A pioneer Kansas woman, Chestina Bowker Allen, recorded in her diary in 1854, "It was a cold blustery day, but we moved into our new house, it consists of two rooms on the lower floor and the attics, we nailed up quilts to make it more comfortable."[6]

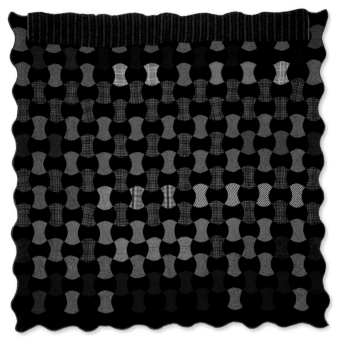

Apple Core, date unknown, made by Nettie J. Bryant, Paonia or Pagosa Springs (or by her mother or grandmother). Wools, hand-pieced and hand-quilted, 77″ × 81″. The top of the quilt has a sleeve to keep a man's beard from soiling the fabric.

"We had good beds and good bedding. Our beds were made of sheepskins, strawticks and featherticks. We had a few good blankets and quilts. We had a buffalo robe. We spent that winter all huddled together with mother around the stove," wrote Mary E. Hatfield LaFollette, who arrived in the Bitterroot Valley of Montana with her parents in 1866. Mary's mother, Mary Jane Hatfield, was a wonder, even in those days when pioneer women sometimes developed skills that would have shocked their eastern sisters. Mary Jane dug post holes, strung wire fence, and roofed the barn by herself. She also performed more feminine duties, such as sewing "with a horsehair, as it would go through the goods and she made many things in this manner. But we had a needle and we were proud of it," her daughter wrote. The needle came in handy when Mary Jane gashed her arm while sliding down a haystack. She sent her husband for her needle and thread and sewed up the gash herself. Her husband fainted.[7]

Most female settlers were far more traditional than Mary Jane Hatfield, although some may have wished to take on male roles. Over a period of several years, Jessie Babcock recorded her life on a farm near Littleton, Colorado. "The boys went hunting. Grandma and Lillie are sewing," Jessie wrote on October 26, 1881. "Papa commenced farming . . .

A Civil War veteran and member of the Grand Army of
the Republic in front of a Nine Patch quilt.

Stars were the most popular 19th century patterns. The back of the photo reads, Mrs. Hartley, Grace and Ruth.

Lillian sewed," she continued in an undated entry in 1884. "Mr. Crotty was here. Lillie sewed. Rained." (June 14, 1884.) "Lillie went to Foxes. I sewed. Pa went to Littleton." (June 25, 1884.) Little surprise, then, that on June 28, 1884, Jessie, then 19, wrote, "Jessie married. I wonder what he wants of me. And how he can care for such a simpleton as I am."[8]

Early Colorado settlers like Jessie took sewing in their stride—along with other events. "One day I had washed up some flour sacks so I could make the children some under clothes," Mrs. Daniel Witter, who settled in Hamilton, Colorado, a gold camp, in 1862, recalled. The same day, she wrote, five hundred Arapaho Indians swarmed around her house and stole her washing, a great loss because "Muslin in those days was a dollar a yard."[9]

With so much work already thrust upon her, Oregon pioneer, business woman, and suffragist Abigail Scott Duniway refused to leave her quilting when unexpected guests arrived. "We had eaten lunch and I had washed the dishes and started work at the quilting frames, when four men came to the cabin. They sat around the fireplace and talked. I replenished the fire and then went ahead with my quilting. After an hour's stay I noticed they were becoming restless. Finally one of them said, 'Well, I guess we might as well go; I don't see any indecisions of dinner.' I was shortly to become a mother."[10]

Abigail might just as well have fed the men, for she disliked sewing and patchwork, and at least one quilt she made was an artistic disaster. In 1900, when she was one of Oregon's best known women, Abigail donated the silk quilt, made up of large sloppy, gaudy hexagons, to the First National Woman Suffrage Bazaar. Believing the quilt, which was thirty years in the making, was historically important, the Portland Woman's Club raised money to buy it for the Oregon Historical Society, a dubious gift. The garish quilt is "acknowledged as not being artistically beautiful or exceptionally well crafted," wrote quilt historian Mary Bywater Cross.[11]

Pioneer journal keeper Nellie Jean Nichols, who worked for a time as postmistress in Vega, Colorado, (now under the Vega Dam) enjoyed her sewing more than Jessie Babcock and Abigail Scott Duniway did and became an accomplished seamstress. She made her elaborate two-piece wool-and-silk wedding dress from a pattern in an 1887 *Godey's Lady's Book*, and her Barn Raising Log Cabin quilt now is in the collection of the Colorado Historical Society. Nellie kept a steady record of her quilting progress:

"I ironed to day and pieced on the quilt," Nellie, then seventeen, wrote on January 22, 1885. . . . "I pieced on the quilt and read. Clarence don't feel well and is cross as an old bear." (January 27, 1885.) "Warm and thawing, I pieced one block for the quilt Granny Jerry brought her dress for Mama to make, it is an awfull botch." (February 3, 1885.) "Warm and pleasant. I pieced two blocks for the quilt. I took the skirt of Mrs. Jerrys dress home this evening—is a 'Daisy' and no mistake." (February 5, 1885.) "I pieced on the quilt—hope I will get it done some time." (February 13, 1885.) "I pieced on the log cabin quilt. Nothing else done." (March 24, 1885.) "We ironed today and pieced on the quilt." (March 25, 1885.) Finally, on March 27, 1885, she wrote, "I finished the log cabin quilt. Will go to church tonight." Less than a week later, the industrious Nellie told her journal, "I started to work some pillow shams." (April 2, 1885.)[12]

An unnamed woman, whose 1883 diary was found in Colorado, records her quilting, along with the joys and sorrows of her life. She probably was close to seventy, because on August 12, 1883, she noted, "One year ago today we celebrated the fiftieth Anniversary of our Marriage."

Her first quilt entry was on February 10, 1883: "We all worked on the quilts. Many done the Saturdays work." On February 12, 1883: "Ann & Mary washed and in the afternoon worked on quilt."

The journal has nearly a dozen quilt entries. "We worked on quilt and Elias leggins. Laura [the writer's daughter?] had sick head-ache and was not able to sit up all day." (February 15, 1883.) "Working on quilt. . . . Laura is some better but miserable yet." (February 16, 1883.) "We are working on the quilt . . . have finished one of Elias leggins. . . . Laura is slim yet." (February 17, 1883.) "Laura a little better. We worked on the bedquilt all day." (February 28, 1883.) "Laura a little better . . . not able to sit up but little. . . . It will be a long time before she will get well. Ann and I take care of her and sew on the quilt." (March 1, 1883.) "We finished up our patch work. . . . The Dr came to night." (March 6, 1883.) That was the journalist's last entry about quilting, perhaps because she had other things, including nursing Laura, to occupy her time. Then comes a heartbreaking entry on May 8, 1883: "Our darling Laura has gone . . . her spirit took its flight at half past eight this evening."[13]

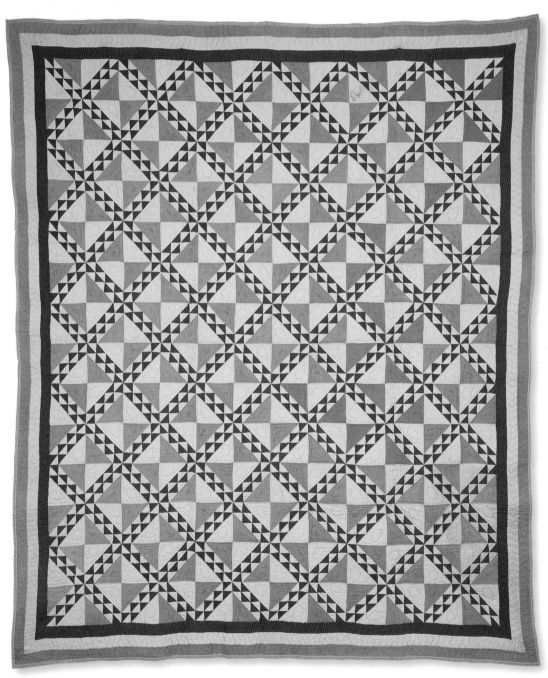

Lady of the Lake, c. 1880, maker unknown. Cottons, machine-pieced and hand-quilted, 65″ × 74″.

The Quilt That Walked to Golden

"Awfull Lonesome"

Many pioneer women found solace in quilting. They enjoyed the respite from chores and remembered easier times as they pieced quilts from old party dresses and worn-out wedding shirts. When "I get lonesome all by myself, I read the names on the pink and white 'Irish Chain' quilt the school children pieced for me," wrote Orpha Baldwin McNitt, who had been a teacher before her move to Evans, Colorado, in 1870.[14] Quietly sewing in the solitude of new homes also caused women to reflect on their lives. "I pieced on the quilt. It is awful lonesome here," Nellie Jean Nichols wrote on January 8, 1885, and again on February 11, 1885: "I pieced on the quilt. Awfull lonesome."[15]

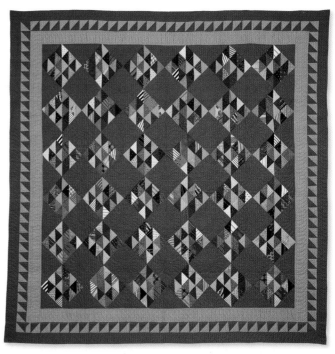

Nine Patch variation, c. 1890, maker unknown. Cotton, machine-pieced and hand-quilted, 91″ × 91″.

In one of his most moving poems, "Magenta," Thomas Hornsby Ferril, Colorado's best-known poet, whose words are in the rotunda of the state capitol in Denver, created a conversation with a dressmaker's dummy he found in a dump of mining machinery in a deserted Gilpin County, Colorado, mining town:

> *The men would measure in cords the gold they hoped*
> *To find, but the women reckoned by calendars*
> *Of double chins and crows-feet at the corners*
> *Of their eyes. When they put their china dishes on*
> *The checkered tablecloth they'd say to themselves*
> *'How soon can we all go away?' When they made quilts*
> *They'd say to the squares of colored cloth 'How soon?'*[16]

Women often saw sewing alone as a diversion from their endless responsibilities. "Sometimes it seemed pleasant to be alone, to sit quietly by the stove, sewing or darning," said Rosie Ise, the seventeen-year-old bride of a German farmer, who moved to western Kansas in 1873. Rosie, whose recollections were written down by her son, John Ise, took her sewing

Shortly after the state was settled, dry goods establishments such as this Colorado store sprang up to provide thread and fabric.

into the cellar when her husband, a justice of the peace, performed unpleasant duties, such as settling disputes. She sewed during other difficult times, and kept her workbasket at her side many years later during her death watch at her husband's bedside.[17]

In an era that offered women few economic opportunities, sewing was a way to raise money for a worthy cause. Catherine Bement, a member of the First United Presbyterian Church of Georgetown, Colorado, formed the Little Willing Workers Society for girls ages five to twelve. "When I was old enough, I became a member of the Little Willing Workers Society and I learned to sew patches for a quilt," one woman recalled. By making quilts, the girls helped raise enough money to buy a chapel that was moved two blocks and attached to their little Gothic stone church as a Sunday school building. The Willing Workers also donated a stained glass window to the church in memory of Mrs. Bement. The window had bees and a beehive on it, "significant of the busy children she had brought together."[18]

Sewing also was an acceptable way for a woman to support herself, as Mollie Sanford found, and it was easier than scrubbing floors and washing clothes. In 1881, Lena Propst, then just fifteen, opened the first dressmaking establishment in Sterling, Colorado. She probably was still at it fifty-seven years later, because her sister Edna wrote, "Lena is still sewing, has her sewing room piled up, and I don't see how she will ever get it all done, but she does and makes her own way. We have too much *pride* to go on any pension."[19]

Lena sewed for fashionable women, and like her eastern counterparts, she probably copied the elaborate designs in *Godey's Lady's Book* and *Peterson's Magazine*. They might have been living on the outskirts of civilization, but western women still wanted to be fashionable. The magazines—books, really—contained uplifting fiction, household hints, and sketches and hand-tinted drawings of the latest fashions, such as winter cloaks, carriage dresses, and frocks suitable to wear to the American Centennial.

Women who performed more pedestrian jobs with their needles found the work less rewarding—and less lucrative. *Emily: The Diary of a Hard-Worked Woman* is an extraordinary journal kept by Emily French, an impoverished working-class Colorado woman, in 1890. Emily, born in 1843, left a worthless husband she referred to as "the old rascal." As a single mother, she was lucky to find any work at all. Fifteen percent of the women in Denver worked in 1890. Most had jobs as domestics, laundresses, or seamstresses, making six dollars a week at most. Emily was not so fortunate. "Sewed for Mrs. Grewell, got nothing but a little bread today," she wrote on June 11, 1890.

Strippy Quilt, 1870–1900, made by Hannah Wilson, Reading, Mich. Velvet upholstery fabrics, machine- and hand-pieced and hand-tied, 62" × 72". Born in England about 1840, Hannah pieced the carriage blanket or sleigh robe after moving to the United States around 1870.

Little Red Schoolhouse, c. 1920, made by Margaret Fay Garrity, Denver, Colo. Cotton, machine-pieced and hand-quilted, 66½" × 85". After her husband died, Margaret lived with various relatives, making quilts for them as payment for room and board.

Emily, who lived in Elbert and Denver as well as the Colorado mountains during the year she kept the diary, did any work she could find, no matter how demeaning or ill-paying. "Picked up the clothes from Mrs[.] Sloans & my own. He put on the boiler, I got her clothes through two waters, then they were so I could put them in to wash. Such clothes are always hard to wash. I have a large lot for us both, 2 quilt for me, 1 for her, flannels &c. I done all by 4, then I cleaned my old chairs, my dishes &c, then my floor which was so verry dirty I scrubbed and rinsed. . . . The pup R. draged & tore the clothes," she wrote on January 10, 1890, when she lived in Elbert, on the Colorado plains. Emily often laundered heavy quilts. "Washed a quilt for Kelleys," she noted on August 12, 1890. And again on October 20, 1890, "I washed a large washing, 2 quilts, 5 sheets, a lot of baby clothes &c." There were her own family's quilts to be laundered, too. "I commenced to wash Annis quilt, it verry dirty," she wrote on June 5, 1890. Annis was Emily's sister. Just a few days later, on June 10, 1890, Emily "washed the Star quilt that Annis gave me for a gift on my 45th birthday."

Despite the heavy load of work she carried, Emily still turned to her needle in her few leisure moments. On a day when she complained to her journal about "my bent shoulders, my crippled hard hands," she "worked on my pillow sham, 'Good morning' and 'Good Night.'"

More often, Emily quilted. On March 31, Emily and Annis "cut blocks to line the log cabin quilt that she is going to piece while I am away. She has made one for a pattern, such a mess. We will see how it will look if she ever does any more to it." Annis apparently did do more to it, because on April 15, Emily "got some blocks, put Annis in her cabin . . ." That done, "went found the colts, drove them in Will Foots corral." Emily also found time to help piece a quilt as a gift. "We must set Dannies quilt together for his present, it is pieced," she wrote on October 11. She thought Dannie would enjoy the quilt, although she knew such handiwork was not always prized. She observed that a neighbor had put a bed quilt on his horse Fanny and remarked that it "must be she has to stand out."

Emily ended her diary on December 31, with her usual recitation of the day's hard work, adding, *"Old Year Goodbye."* That is our good-bye to Emily, too, since there is no record of what happened to her. Like the quilts she worked and hand-washed, Emily French may simply have worn out.[20]

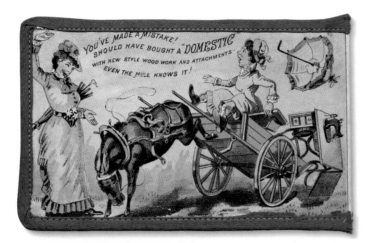

By 1860, sewing machines were for sale in Colorado.

"The Simplest Singer on the Market"

A sewing machine, of course, would have made Emily French's life easier, and she mentions in her journal on May 6, 1890, "I went again then to see about getting the sewing machine" although she doesn't mention whether she was successful.[21] Emily knew a machine could do in minutes what would take her hours to accomplish. The first patent on such a machine had been taken out in England in 1790, nearly seventy years before the Colorado gold rush, and a similar machine was invented in the United States in 1834 by Walter Hunt (who also invented the safety pin). But it was not until the Civil War that this labor-saving device made its first inroads into American households. A machine made by I.M. Singer & Company in 1850 sold for $125, but by 1870, the price of a Singer had been halved to $64. Some do-gooders feared a machine that stitched, saying it would drive poor seamstresses out of work, something that failed to happen, of course.[22] Although women found the contraption let them make quilts quickly, purists decried the use of machine stitches. In *Old Quilts*, quilt historian William Rush Dunton, Jr. described the fine stitching in an 1940s Album quilt top where some of the pieces were barely a quarter of an inch. "Try to sew that on your electric sewing machine, Mrs. Twentieth Century," he sniffed.[23] Emily French probably intended to borrow a sewing machine. She didn't have the money to purchase one. Other women were more fortunate. "I bought me a sewing machine last week," Maggie Brown proudly wrote to her father in Virginia in 1882. Maggie and her husband, Charles, a physician, lived in Bonanza, a Colorado mining town.[24]

Another woman, this one in Idaho, also shared with her father her excitement over a new sewing machine, bought with her earnings from washing clothes for neighbors. "Father, would you believe that your 'washer woman' has a wonderful new piece of furniture? A sewing machine! Think of it! The simplest Singer on the market and it cost $72. . . . It was freighted with an ox team from Corinne to Eagle Rock. It surely is an acquisition and my friends come from miles around to have

Sewing was either an endless task or a respite from housekeeping drudgery.

me sew for them. They gladly do all of the drudgery around the house if I will just condescend to put machine stitching on their hems," Emma Just wrote to her father in England in 1874. Still, even her time-saving sewing machine couldn't keep Emma from feeling overwhelmed at times. Two years later, she told her father of the birth of her fourth child, "more of a family than her mother ever had. . . . Surely no mother should be called upon to wash and cook and sew for more than four."[25]

Jennie Marcy, who moved to Kansas in 1877 and lived on a farm near Baldwin City, described sitting at her sewing machine in front of a window, "working her feet 'like a house o' fire' treading the little old Grovner-Baker sewing machine, an ancient low-armed contraption, but still 'the latest improved model'—oh yes, a little larger than a coffee-mill and a trifle higher than a milking stool."[26]

After her husband, a freighter, was killed by Sioux Indians near Kearney, Nebraska, Marietta Narcissis Emily Gorton, who was left behind in Missouri, lost his entire estate, including six farms, to an unscrupulous lawyer. Left with several children and a sewing machine, she made quilts and sold them to people traveling west in wagon trains. Marrying James Jacob Wilson, Emily herself went west to Wyoming, where she lived in a sod house. When Indians showed up unexpectedly, Emily fed them, hoping they would spare her family's life. The Indians not only did not molest Emily's family, but several days afterward, they left a slain deer on her doorstep. Later Emily made quilts out of old shirts and traded them to the Indians.

Eventually, Emily moved to Hereford, where she made pieced and tied quilts that she sold for $10 to $15 each. She used a quilt frame made with one- by three-inch boards, held together with wooden pins. The frame was set up on the backs of chairs.

In 1887, a well-to-do woman might have an elaborate mahogany sewing stand.

Picnickers in Greeley, Colorado, use a quilt for a tablecloth.

"She said a quilt was sewed together with love. When you passed it on to your neighbor, you were passing on your love. It was a special thing to give to a neighbor, like putting your arms around someone and giving them a love," said her great-granddaughter, Pat Hubbard. "When Grandmother was upset or had problems, you found her sitting there, humming old Christian songs and quilting." Emily Wilson passed her love of sewing on to Pat, who remembered sitting under the quilt frame as her great-grandmother tied quilts, telling the older woman when the needle came through the fabric. Today, Pat Hubbard is a nationally acclaimed quilter, known for her story quilts in which she often stitches her family heritage.[27]

Women who didn't have their own sewing machines often took their work to more fortunate neighbor women who owned the contraptions. "The Bartsches had the only one in the neighborhood, and it was about worn out. Once when Rosie [Ise] was making a dress with bias folds on the skirt, Henry suggested that she let him take the dress up to Mary Bartsch to have Mary sew the bias pieces on her machine. Rosie readily assented, but the machine puckered the folds so badly that the dress was hardly fit to wear. She paid fifty cents for the work too—a cent a yard for the stitching," John Ise wrote about his Kansas mother. The cost was dear, since Rosie was frugal. She was bitterly disappointed when she discovered that the bargain cloth she bought from an itinerant peddler turned out to be cheap shoddy, and she once denied herself a snack of cheese at the general store when she realized the same amount of money bought a spool of thread. The thread would be used for patching, the spool strung with others to make a child's toy. When Rosie finally got her own sewing machine, the neighbors brought their sewing to her, paying her by washing dishes or doing farm chores. "The sewing machine was in a real sense a community institution," wrote Ise.[28]

Some lucky women not only owned sewing machines, but hired seamstresses to come in and do their sewing. In her autobiography, *Father Struck It Rich*, Evalyn Walsh McLean remembered, "Every spring and fall a spinster, Miss Ewing, came to the Vine Street house [in Denver] to make dresses. The living room became the sewing room and Vinson [Evalyn's brother] and I had fun teasing Miss Ewing. Cautioned to leave her alone, we turned stealthy. She discovered that her sewing machine would not operate. I had put chewing gum in the works." Evalyn's father, Thomas Walsh, discovered the fabulously rich Camp Bird Mine near Ouray, Colorado. Evalyn, who grew up to be what in those days was known as a madcap, married Ned McLean, whose family owned the *Washington Post* and the *Cincinnati Enquirer*, became a confidante of Presidents, and bought the Hope Diamond.[29]

Sewing machines led to a gold mine of sorts for Elizabeth Sarah Fraser, who came to Colorado in 1868 as a representative of the Singer Manufacturing Company (successor company of I.M. Singer). Lizzie Fraser was not the first sewing machine saleswoman in Colorado. That distinction goes to a woman whose name comes down only as Mrs. L.E. Miller. In 1860, Mrs. Miller arrived in the city in an ox-drawn covered wagon with a sample sewing machine hauled from Berlin, Wisconsin, and sold models for as much as $160.[30]

Some eight years later, Lizzie Fraser set up a Singer sales office in the News Building on Larimer Street in Denver.[31] The year before, Singer had passed its rival, Wheeler and Wilson, in sales and was on its way to dominating the sewing machine market.[32] Lizzie

*Washington Sidewalk variation, 1899, made by "Egbert **Ramsey** Great Grandmother Finkell" (**label on quilt**). Cottons, hand-pieced and hand-quilted, 74" × 84½".*

The Quilt That Walked to Golden

ran frequent advertisements in the *Rocky Mountain News* for "Our New Family SEWING MACHINE . . . THE BEST SEWING MACHINE In Existence, L.S. Fraser, Agent for Colorado.[33] She was offered a job as treasurer of Singer in Chicago in 1869, but in 1870, she married widower John Iliff, a wealthy banker and cattleman. Singer gave her a pearl-inlaid sewing machine as a wedding present. (It now resides in the Bloom Mansion in Trinidad, Colorado. Owned by the Colorado Historical Society, the Bloom Mansion was the family home of Alberta Bloom Iliff, John Iliff's daughter-in-law.) John Iliff died in 1878, and five years later, Lizzie married Henry Warren, a bishop in the Methodist Church. In later years, Lizzie's step-granddaughter Alberta Iliff Shattuck recalled, Lizzie did not sew but instead hired a seamstress to come in twice a year to make clothes for her and her daughters.[34]

Working Girls

Since almost all western women plied their needles in some fashion, it seems likely that prostitutes sewed, although there is no mention of their doing so in any of the social histories about the West. When researching the lives of these working girls, historians probably didn't pay a whole lot of attention to needlework. Nonetheless, the women had dresses to mend, and perhaps when the garments were too far gone, the prostitutes ripped them up for quilts. Racy views produced for stereopticons show unscrupulous women going through men's pockets while the men sleep under quilts, so it's possible that the prostitutes kept quilts on their beds, although common sense says a woman wouldn't want to put a great deal of time into making a precious quilt that could be spoiled in one evening by a customer's spurs or muddy boots.

Still, some prostitutes apparently used everyday quilts. Several years after the Dumas, the last operating brothel in Butte, Montana, was shut down in 1982, a new owner cleaned out the basement. The

Whether the Old Homestead, Cripple Creek's finest brothel, ever had hand-made quilts on the beds is anybody's guess. Gentlemen clients of the parlor house, shown in the 1950s after it was turned into a museum, didn't visit to look at the bedspreads.

Sugans

Cowboys prepare to bed down under their sugans.

If the Mountain West made a contribution to American quilting, it is the *sugan*—also soogan, soogin, suggan, sugin, or sougan—a crude, undersize quilt used by cowboys and "gyppos," as independent loggers in the Northwest were called. A sugan, derived from an Irish word, was also known as a "parker" or a "henskin" when it was stuffed with feathers.[i] Elsewhere, it was known as a hired man's quilt. Usually made of large patches cut from pants and coats, the sugan often was tied rather than quilted, and it weighed about four pounds—"a pound for each corner."[ii] It could be square and "'drove cowboys crazy' trying to decide which was length and which was breadth, as the saying went."[iii]

In fact, sugans drove everybody crazy. "We had all these big—they called them sugans—quilts, and they were made out of old overalls and old clothes, old woolen coats, you know, patchwork quilts, and then there would be a batt, a cotton batt in between," remembered Jennie Brown Spence, who slept under one during a fall roundup near Meeker, Colorado. "We had about three of them over us, and I couldn't turn over. They weren't eiderdown, like they are today, or sleeping bags. It was just those heavy sugans."[iv]

The sugans were a source of mirth for cowboys, who loved practical jokes. They would tell greenhorns they had slept in a bed "infested with soogins." One visitor, recalled Agnes Morley Cleaveland, who grew up on a New Mexico ranch, got the last laugh on the cowboy prankster and retorted, "You should laugh. I happen to know that you slumber in your bed." The enraged cowboy told him, "No man can say that about me and git off with it." The other hands hustled the visitor off before the cowboy could find his gun.[v]

i Winfred Blevins, *Dictionary of the American West*, (New York: Facts On File, 1993,) 351. Ramon F. Adams, *Cowboy Lingo*, (Boston: Houghton Mifflin Co., 2000,) 34–5, and *Western Words: A Dictionary of the American West*, (Norman: University of Oklahoma Press, 1968,) 220, 311.
ii Ramon F. Adams, *Western Words: A Dictionary of the American West*, 311.
iii Agnes Morley Cleaveland, *No Life for a Lady*, (Boston: Houghton Mifflin Co., 1941. Reprint Lincoln: University of Nebraska Press, 1977,) 166.
iv Julie Jones-Eddy, ed., *Homesteading Women: An Oral History of Colorado 1890–1950*, (New York: Twayne Publishers, 1992,) 63.
v Agnes Morley Cleaveland, *No Life for A Lady*, 166.

two-story Dumas, on Butte's Venus Alley in the heart of the red-light district, had been built as a whorehouse, with long hallways down the center of each floor and small rooms opening off them. Each room had a window that looked out onto the hall so that a girl could display herself when she wasn't otherwise occupied. The basement also had cribs opening off a center hallway, but the cellar was dank and had been closed up since 1943.

Prior to turning the Dumas into a museum, the new owner tackled the basement, and there among bobby pins and gum wrappers, Camel and Old Gold packages, opium bottles and hand-made whips, were five quilts. They were simple and poorly made, and it was clear that they had been well-used. One is nothing more than squares of woolen clothing tacked to batting and back. The most elaborate is a Nine Patch made of 1930s fabrics, with small nine-patches for the center and corner squares and strip blocks for the alternating patches. There are no records of who made the quilts, of course. Perhaps they were pieced by mothers or sisters, unaware of the girl's occupation and the use to which they would be put. Or the prostitutes themselves could have made them.[35] In the early part of the century, the Venus Alley prostitutes sat in their windows knitting, tapping on the glass with their needles to attract the attention of prospective clients.[36] So Butte's working girls may have been more industrious than prostitutes in, say, New York.

In his weighty 1897 tome, *The History of Prostitution*, Dr. William W. Sanger noted that New York prostitutes "generally indulge in a luxurious indolence" when they had no visitors. "For any useful employment, such as even sewing or fancy needlework, they have but little inclination, and their general refuge from *ennui* is found in reading novels." A girl had to do something to pass the time between tricks, as the Butte soiled doves had learned, and not all of them could read. German prostitutes were somewhat more ambitious, Dr. Sanger noted. They "engaged in knitting or sewing; for German girls, whether virtuous or prostitute, seem to have a horror of idleness, and even in such a place as this are seldom seen without their work."[37]

Such Quilts!

Western women also had a horror of idleness, and they spent their new-found leisure time showing off their sewing skills. In the late nineteenth century, most women sewed. Many girls still learned at their mothers' knees, but a growing number were taught sewing in public school. During the 1897–1898 school year, Maggie Jennings, a student at Manual Training High School in Denver, put together a two-volume sewing book, probably for her

Dutch Rose, 1900–1925, made by Virginia America Stover. Cottons, hand-pieced and hand-quilted, 71″ × 86½″. Virginia was an African American who made many quilts.

The Quilt That Walked to Golden

home economics class. The book began with samples of basting stitches, then went on to show hem-stitching and feather-stitching. Once she mastered the stitches, Maggie made miniature plackets and drawers and gored skirts. In her neat girlish hand, Maggie wrote sewing instructions and handy hints: "Never bite thread, always cut or break it. For ordinary sewing the thread should be the length of the arm.... The correct position for sewing is to sit upright, with the shoulders thrown back and feet on the floor."[38]

Maggie had no quilt patterns in her school book, but her elders still measured their sewing skills by their quilts. And "Such quilts!" wrote India Simmons, who arrived in Kansas in 1887. "Appliqued patterns of flowers and ferns, put on with stitches so dainty as to be almost invisible, pieced quilts in basket or sugarbowl or intricate star pattern, each one quilted with six or more spools of thread, the patterns of the quilting brought out in bare relief by padding with cotton each leaf or petal or geometric design; soft, fleecy, home-woven blankets; linens woven from their own flax and embroidered deep in scalloped and cut-out-designs."[39]

By the time the nineteenth century drew to a close, in fact, western women were the equals of their quilt-making sisters in the East. They saved fragile scraps of silk, satin, and velvet, yellow cigar bands, and commemorative ribbons to make quilts that were more show than bedcover. Margaret Geick, great-granddaughter of Mary Jane Burgess, the woman responsible for the quilt dubbed The Quilt That Walked to Golden, remembered that her family had a Log Cabin quilt made with silk fabrics salvaged by a friend who did alterations at one of Denver's finest clothing stores, possibly Gano-Downs Company.[40]

In 1877, Emma Schoefield Wright, daughter of the president of the Burlington Northern Railroad, began collecting signatures of famous Americans—politicians, religious leaders, and suffragists—who signed their names on scraps of silk. Signatures included Ulysses S. Grant, Chester Arthur, Admiral George Dewey, and the Archbishop of Canterbury. Then Emma fashioned a Tumbling Blocks autograph quilt from the signatures, adding her own pen-and-ink sketches to the blank patches. The quilt, now owned by the Colorado Historical Society, was insured in its day for $3,000—about $57,000 today. It was shown in art exhibits across the country.[41]

Far from the fashion centers of the East, Colorado stitchers nonetheless were caught up in the mania for crazy quilts. Quilt historians in the first half of the twentieth century thought them horrid. The use of embroidery on patchwork quilts "marks a decadent step," shuddered William Rush Dunton, Jr. in *Old Quilts*.[42] Still, women found crazy quilts a perfect showcase for their skill with a needle. Was there a fashionable home in Denver, Colorado Springs, or Pueblo that didn't have a quilt, throw, or pillow made of gaudy scraps of rich fabrics and embroidered with fancy stitches? "Instead of being the humblest of bed-coverings, [the crazy quilt] was promoted to parlor lounge as the last word in 'slumber throw' elegance. No home of average comfort was complete without its crazy-patch slumber throw, elaborately pieced of odds and ends of ribbons, silks and velvets, all feather-stitched together or even more fancifully embroidered," wrote Ruth E. Finley in her 1929 work, *Old Patchwork Quilts and the Women Who Made Them*.[43]

Women loved posing in front of their quilts, especially crazy quilts.

Colorado women pieced together fragile patches of silk, satin, and velvet that had been cut into a hodge-podge of shapes, then embroidered the seams in a variety of stitches. They embroidered designs such as flowers, animals, and their initials on the scraps or covered them with charming pen-and-ink sketches. Crazy quilts were often made to mark a special occasion or were given as gifts, a little like the friendship quilts that had been presented to pioneer women before their journey west.

A group of Colorado church women fashioned a silk, satin, and velvet crazy quilt, trimmed with gold-and-maroon silk cord and tassels, and gave it to the wife of Governor Benjamin Harrison Eaton. "Presented to Mrs. Eaton by the Ladies of the Boulevard Congregational church Assisted by the Legislators of 1885" was written in gold paint on a maroon velvet patch.[44] Florence Bell, a black woman in Denver, spent three years making a silk quilt embroidered with tennis racquets, balls, and a net, along with figures, such as two Asian women. Born a slave, Florence, who lived from

String Star, 1917, made by Isa Shamon, Partridge, Kans. Wools, hand-pieced and hand-quilted, 70″ × 79″.

Crazy Quilt with Sixteen Patch, 1889, maker unknown. Cotton, hand- and machine-pieced and hand-tied, 80" × 80". Many of the blocks contain names or initials signed in ink. The reverse side, worked in Sixteen Patch, is shown opposite.

The Quilt That Walked to Golden

1852 to 1895, used 318 spools of silk on the quilt, which she finished in 1893.[45] In presenting it to the Colorado Historical Society, Florence's husband, John L. Bell, said that Florence was born a slave and was "a self Maide womman."[46]

Several years earlier, Augusta Tabor, the unfortunate first wife of Colorado's silver king, the woman who had made the tent her family slept in when they came to Colorado in 1859, completed a crazy quilt. It was made up of silk and satin scraps she had collected for thirty years. She had put aside some of the fabrics even before her marriage to H.A.W. Tabor in Maine in 1857, and brought them west with her. Augusta combined the scraps with souvenir ribbons and the silk program for the Grand March of Leadville's Tabor Hose Company #5. She added patches that had been hand-painted by her sister, Mary Marston, an Augusta, Maine, artist, and embroidered scraps that had been worked for her by friends. Augusta did her own embroidery, too, memo-

An African-American woman poses with a crazy quilt with fans in the corners

rializing family members, as well as herself. The 97″ × 123″ spread, now in the textiles collection of the Colorado Historical Society, was completed with a patch embroidered "Mrs. A. Tabor," and the date, "January 5, 1885."[47] By then, Tabor had divorced Augusta to marry Baby Doe. The quilt proved more enduring than Augusta's marriage.

Hazel Green, whose 1885–1886 diary, written in a composition book, was found in Colorado, recorded "my 83rd birth day darke and dreary." Little wonder, then, that she brooded over what to do with her most beloved possessions. On the last page of the journal, she specified, "My small rocking Chair I wish for Friend Libbie to have with all that is on it, My Craze Quilt is for Libbie too."[48]

Hands All Around

"I like hands—sewing hands, especially my own, willing and faithful."

Anne Ellis

Women always had come together to sew, and as soon as they were settled, industrious Colorado pioneer women took their sewing with them whenever they visited. Sewing bees gave isolated women a sense of community, a feeling of civilization and refinement even in remote mining towns like Bonanza, where residents were often impoverished. "It was the custom, then [1880s], for the women to go visiting and stay all day. Our place was a great hold-out, as Mama was a good cook, always glad to have them, very entertaining, laughing at and with them," wrote Anne Ellis in *The Life of an Ordinary Woman.*

Dutch Tulips, c. 1930, maker unknown, Winnetoon, Neb. Cottons, hand-appliqued, machine-pieced and hand-quilted, 71½″ × 88″.

Eighteen pieced quilts is an impressive output. The quilt block above the woman's head is
Hands All Around.

Such visits were expected to be reciprocal, of course. Anne's mother, who made all her children's clothing, including her sons' suits, hooked rugs, and pieced quilts, was poor and illiterate, but she was proud, and she knew social niceties. While living in Bonanza, she decided to return the call of a Mrs. Rayworth, "who was a frosty-nosed sort of a person [who] came oftener than most, and was given of our best; so one day Mama . . . taking the two youngest and her sewing she walked the mile to town, arriving tired and a little cross. Mrs. Rayworth does not seem any too glad to see her." Anne's mother "gets out her sewing and prepares for a visit. She sits and sits, till it is time to start dinner, but nothing stirs; dinner time comes, still nothing doing (the children growing restless and Mama with her stomach clinging to her backbone); afternoon comes,

Shoofly.

but no mention is made of eating. Then Mama can stand it no longer, so bundles up her sewing and children and walks the mile home, hot and hungry." The next day, Mrs. Rayworth showed up at Anne's mother's house with a friend, but as the two came through her gate, Anne's mother met them with "blood in her eye, saying, 'Stop right in your tracks; you ain't comin' in here. . . . The gall of you! Never so much as offering me a drink of water. If you don't hit the trail pretty soon, my dander is going to raise.' "[1]

Sewing, Anne Ellis summed up in another book, *Plain Anne Ellis: More About the Life of an Ordinary Woman*, one of three autobiographies she wrote, "is like everything else—each day brings its achievements, its disappointments, its funny side, and its tragedy." Despite the books' titles, Anne was an extraordinary woman. Growing up poor in Bonanza, she was widowed as a young woman and led a hand-to-mouth existence as she struggled to support her children in the mining towns of the West. One of Anne's jobs was dressmaking, something she knew little about when she started in the early twentieth century, but quickly learned. "I sewed good wishes and thoughts into my garments, especially so if they were wedding or graduation dresses. I like hands—sewing hands, especially my own, willing and faithful," she wrote.

"Sewing is like everything else, it has its good and its bad side—the good far exceeding the bad," continued Anne. Nonetheless, life as a seamstress had plenty of bad moments, and Anne might have thought nostalgically of her mother's sewing bees. Anne remembered a time when she planned to buy a steak for her family for dinner, using the money earned from making a dress. Her son, in fact, was poised to run to the store the minute his mother handed him the cash. But when the customer picked up the dress, she told

Although commercial yarn was readily available by the turn of the twentieth century, some women still spun their own.

Anne, "I can't pay you for a week or two. I spent all my money for new records." Anne held her tongue, saying only that she thought the woman would look good in the dress. Then Anne remarked in the book, "It was red, and she had pimples."[2]

Once, when papering her walls with newspaper, Anne came across the couplet:

> *Sometimes I stop with half-drawn thread,*
> *Not often, though—each moment's time means bread.*[3]

Eventually, Anne tired of dressmaking. "The thought of sewing all summer was too much for me," she wrote. Perhaps she disliked the loneliness of sewing by herself, too. She found a job at a sheep camp in the mountains, feeding the sheep shearers for fifty cents a meal. It was easier work.[4]

Soft Shucks for Comfort

In the early twentieth century, women found quilts and quiltmaking as important as ever. They thought in terms of quilts. "Here runs a patchwork street with new on old," wrote Belle Turnbull, a Breckenridge poet, in "Window on the Street."[5] Belle used stitchery to give mystery to a character. "What does she want, thought Dorn, What does she smile about above her needle," Belle wrote in *Goldboat*, her epic poem about gold dredging in Summit County.[6]

Although store-bought spreads and mattresses were becoming common by 1900, women continued to make bedding. "The folks bought a few geese, so Mom would have feathers for pillows and feather beds," remembered Allen Bright, who was a member of a Bent County pioneer family.[7] Gladys Smith Nelson, another Colorado pioneer woman, recalled a neighbor who hired men to shuck corn. "The soft shucks were used for mattresses," she

Twinkling Stars, c. 1930, made by Alice Melum Moss, Evanston, Ill. Cottons, hand-pieced and hand-quilted, 59½" × 91". Alice didn't have room in her house for a quilt frame, so she sent the top to South Carolina to be quilted by a church group.

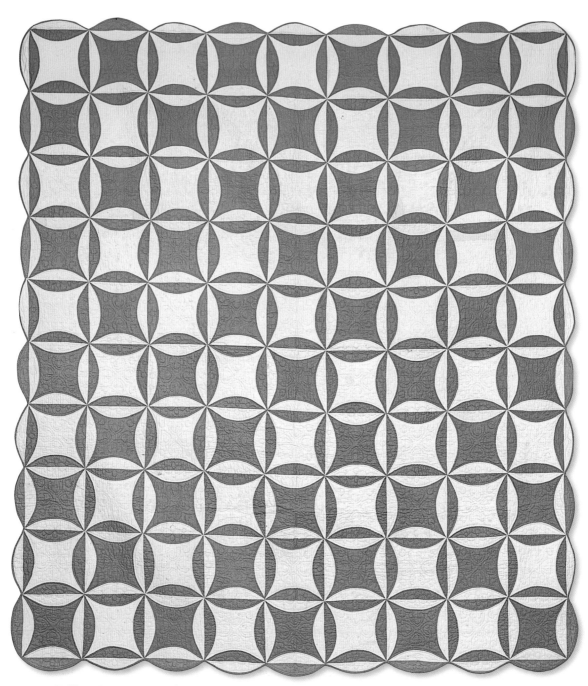

Robbing Peter to Pay Paul or Orange Peel, c. 1930, maker unknown. Cottons, machine-pieced and hand-quilted, 80″ × 89½″.

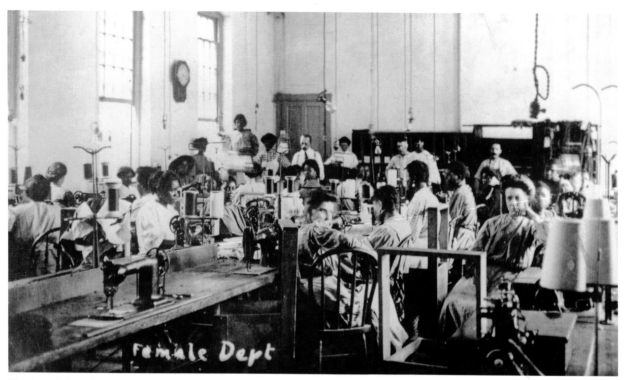

Black and white female convicts learn sewing in the state penitentiary in Cañon City.

said.[8] Other families stuffed ticks with whatever was available to them. "I didn't always have a mattress, but Mom would make me a straw tick, which was nice and soft and just great to sleep on. She made all of our quilts, the best ones were always for the bed spread and the others were to keep you warm. When she made me a new dress she would always save any leftover pieces for quilt scraps. When she finished a quilt, it was always fun to look for the ones that I had dresses made of," wrote Lee Kloepfer about her days in Ouray, Colorado, a mining town.[9]

"There were no springs—just slats, a straw-filled tick, cotton blankets and cotton batting comforters. These Mother made," wrote Hazel W. Dalziel, who grew up on a farm near Longmont at the turn of the century. "The tops were pieced out of scraps of material, sometimes wool but mostly cotton. The back was a length of lightweight cotton-material. This was stretched over four long wooden slats which were made to form a square and nailed at the corners."[10]

Corn shuck and straw ticks on bedsteads might have been preferable to the pallets made from quilts stacked on the floor of a house where a mail carrier and his family

Mexican Star.

slept on their first night in Arriba, Colorado, on the eastern plains. "Suddenly a shriek from the youngest girl, me, awakened the entire household. The parents, with lantern in hand, raced upstairs in time to see a rat escaping through the hole in the lathes . . . and saw teeth marks and missing skin from the tip of my nose," recalled Marjorie Nelson, who was three years old at the time.[11]

Rodents weren't the only creature threats to sleepers. "One day Mom saw little red spots all over me," Lois Flansburg Haaglund wrote in her western memoir, *Tough, Willing, and Able: Tales of a Montana Family*. "On investigation she found bedbugs in my bed. Horrified, she tore into the house. She yanked back the rear wall tarp and slung out every old sugan that had been lugged in from various logging camps by Dad's brothers and friends. She scrubbed down everything in the room and washed every piece of clothing and bedding in the house. She sprinkled bedbug dust liberally in all the corners, nooks, and niches. She set cans filled with bug powder under each bed leg. Then she designated one day a week as 'Bedbug Day.' She got rid of 'em."[12]

More often than not, however, quilts were a source of comfort. When the family Ford broke down on a lonely Montana road, Georgia Schad recalled, "Mother, who was always prepared, brought forth quilts and blankets that she had tucked away. We divided these up and though we were without food and water we made comfortable beds in the warm sand beside our stranded Ford."[13] Alice Cora Dickerson, whose family homesteaded near Eaton, Colorado, remembered that in cold weather, "rocks heated on a campfire were wrapped and placed at [teamsters'] feet and they snuggled in a quilt wrapped around them," not only to keep warm but to actually stay alive. Alice's own bed was cozier. She and her sister slept year-around in a screened-in porch with a canvas curtain to keep out the snow. Despite the cold, the girls rolled back the curtain so that they could see the stars. "Snow blew in on the floor and bed and there would be frost on our faces and hair" in the morning, Alice said.[14]

Sewing bees, such as this one in Colorado Springs, became popular as women had more leisure.

"The Comfort of the Inner Woman"

With the coming of the new century, Colorado was no longer the frontier. Named a state in 1876—the Centennial State—Colorado was filling up. By 1900, it had a population of 540,000. Manufacturing and services had joined mining and agriculture as important economic sectors. Colorado's major cities—Denver, Colorado Springs, and Pueblo—were filled with office structures, civic buildings, and mansions. While many Colorado families still lived in isolated areas, with attendant hardships, more and more Coloradoans were residents of towns and cities. They were better off financially than the previous generation, and the increased affluence, along with the growth of domestic labor-saving devices, such as washing machines, electric lights, and gas stoves, not to mention cheap sewing machines, gave women more leisure time to sew.

Some women, of course, used their wealth to avoid sewing altogether. In an engagements book kept during 1907 and 1908, an unnamed Denver society woman wrote nary a word about sewing herself, much less quilting. "Shopping," she begins her first entry in the diary, December 9, 1907. And later: "sewing girl. 2 hours." (December 14, 1907.) Other entries tell of her weekly "Lesson Français," social events with prominent Denver families in their homes or at Elitch Gardens (an amusement park with theater and flower gardens), or meetings of the National Society of the Colonial Dames of America and National Society Daughters of the American Revolution.[15]

Other women spent time sewing instead of gadding about. "I generally pieced blocks. I never pieced very many quilts. I think three nice [quilts.] I always put in wool. We had sheep . . . I generally clipped the wool off myself and washed it. I didn't know how to card it, but I just kind of pulled it apart and placed it together and made a mat out of it—batt, we called them . . . then I quilted it. I still have them. I sleep on it every winter. I put it under my sheets in the wintertime. And a wool quilt on top of me," Hilda Shelton Rawlinson told a researcher. Born in 1905, Hilda was raised in Maybell, and later lived with her husband on a ranch near Meeker.[16]

"Grandmother came to live with us in the 1920s. She quilted little bitty old pieces, quilted quite a little for other people. We had a neighbor with five daughters, and she had a lot of pieces, and she asked my grandmother to piece on shares," said Ila Small Lingelbach. In 1913, at the age of five, Ila and her family moved from Nebraska to a homestead in northeast Colorado. Her mother and grandmother propped up a big quilt frame

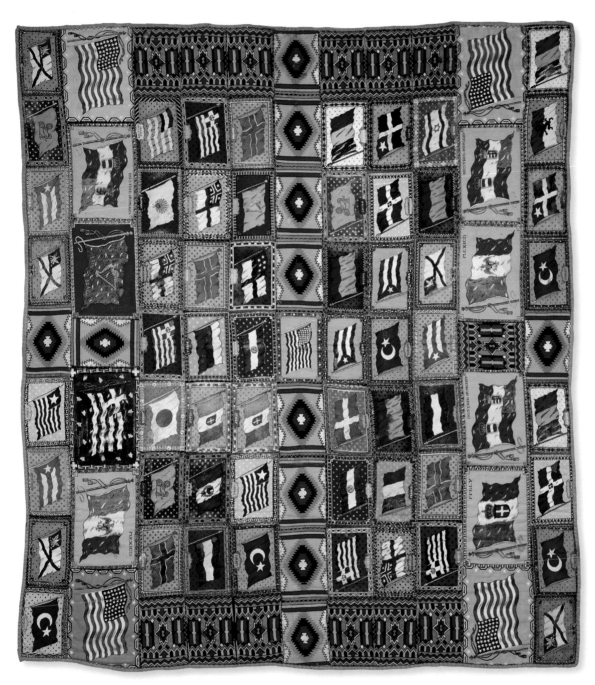

Tobacco Flag, c. 1915, possibly made by (?) Brumbaugh. Cottons, machine-pieced and tacked by hand-embroidery, 64" × 71¼". Flannel flags were given as premiums in cigarette packages about 1915. Eugenia Mitchell bought the quilt for $60 from a woman who needed the money for groceries.

Girls at the Denver Orphans' Home were taught domestic skills.

on chairs in the main room of the homestead, which annoyed Ila's father, because he had to crawl under it to go to bed.[17]

By quilting on shares—making a top for a neighbor in exchange for fabric—Ila's grandmother acquired material without having to buy it. Other women made do, too. "We dyed some sacks pale green and orange to put some quilts together with. Used green and a brownish orange edge. It is quite pretty," Stella Dickerson wrote to her daughter Alice from Eggers, Colorado, February 17, 1932.[18] Contemporary Colorado quilter Pat Hubbard said her great-grandmother saved Bull Durham tobacco sacks, soaked them to get rid of the paper stickers, dyed them, and cut them into shapes for quilts. Her grandmother also utilized feedsacks for quilt pieces.[19]

Feedsacks were a common source of fabric for dressmakers and quilters, as manufacturers knew. "We always tried to get two or three of the same pattern so we could

The Quilt That Walked to Golden

make dresses out of them," said Ila Lingelbach. Sugar and flour manufacturers sold their products in colorful sacks as well as bags printed with the company name. Frugal seamstresses also made use of these logo-emblazoned sacks for their sewing. They became quilt backing, since the printed names wouldn't show on the underside of a quilt. Or they were bleached and dyed and cut up for quilt pieces. "Some brands of flour were easier to get [the printing] out. Belle of Denver was harder. I remember one girl when she'd swing, you could see 'Belle of Denver' across the seat of her pants. She was called the Belle of Denver," Ila Lingelbach recalled in a classic feedsack story.[20]

Margaret Geick's grandmother, Margaret Tucker Burgess, used the undersides of shirt collars for quilt pieces. Margaret Burgess was an outstanding quilter who, with her daughter, Marion Burgess Geick, made a red-and-green National Recovery Act quilt, using the NRA eagle. They began the quilt August 23, 1931, and finished it in 1933, according to notations on the quilt, using as a quilting pattern oak leaves gathered in Left Hand Canyon, near Boulder. Even such accomplished quilters as these could be tripped up. The two made a colorful applique quilt with birds and trees. Only after finishing the quilt did they discover that the fabric was not colorfast. They named it Heartbreak Quilt.[21]

Another imaginative quilter was Theresa Walter Haaf, who lived for a time in Colorado Springs. She collected signatures of famous people for a celebrity or album quilt that is in the collection of the Colorado Springs Pioneers Museum. Among the ninety-six Americans who signed the muslin blocks that Theresa sent to them were politicians, writers, inventors, and musicians. They included Herbert Hoover, Pearl Buck, Walt Disney, Mary Pickford, George Bernard Shaw, Albert Einstein, and John Ringling. Mary embroidered the signatures in turkey red, then used an unthreaded sewing machine to mark her stitching design. She quilted the blocks separately and tatted them together.[22]

Crazy Quilt, 1919–1922, made by Angie Naomi Rideout, Colorado. Wools, foundation-pieced by hand and hand-embroidered, 67″ × 80½″. Angie made the quilt in five pieces so that she could hold one on her lap while she sewed by the light of a coal oil lamp. The quilt contains the initials of Angie's family.

Colorado quilters showed western pride by picking patterns that related to the state. A popular one among pioneer women was called Rocky Mountain, which is known elsewhere as New York Beauty. From the early 1900s until mid-century, magazines and pattern books printed patterns with Colorado themes, including Colorado Beauty (*Comfort*), Colorado (*Hearth and Home*), The Great Divide (*The Ladies Home Journal*), Springtime in the Rockies (*Capper's Weekly*), and Pikes Peak (*Practical Needlework Patterns*).[23]

Women quilted alone, but with more leisure time and better transportation, they came together for afternoons of sewing. Quilting bees "were a purely American social custom, unknown in foreign countries," according to historian William Rush Dunton, Jr., author of the classic, *Old Quilts*. A self-described "physician to nervous ladies," Dr.

Contained Crazy Quilt, c. 1940, made by (?) Ericson. Rayons and silks, machine-pieced, hand-embroidered, and hand-quilted, 73″ × 73″. The maker owned a mercantile store in Chicago and may have made the quilt with coat-lining fabric.

Dunton found something psychological in quilting bees. "With several nervous ladies working on similarly patterned blocks for a quilt there naturally arises a spirit of competition or rivalry, to produce the best made block. This is also a healthy mental attitude and is the beginning of a community spirit, which is increased by joining the blocks and participating in the quilting, usually a merry occasion, with many quips and jokes bandied about. If interest can be stimulated in quilt making it affords a valuable means of restoring healthy thought." The good doctor theorized that cutting out quilt pieces helped restore inmates of mental institutions to sanity or at least, kept them from getting worse.[24]

While more than one woman probably picked up her needle to keep from going nuts, most women didn't become communal sewers to restore mental health through competition. They joined quilting bees because they wanted to socialize and enjoy themselves—and to show off their sewing as well as their culinary skills. "Our readers must not think that these feminine pastimes are a thing of the past. The old custom, hallowed by fond memories[,] is still observed; and Saturday Mrs. H.L. Wyman entertained a num-

B.B. Freeman moved his family onto this hardscrabble farm near Grand Junction in 1908. Five years later, a government canal brought water for irrigation—and for washing quilts.

Quilt of Many Colors, c. 1935, made by Bessie Bailey Sanford Sutton Henderson, Michigan. Cottons, hand-pieced and hand-quilted, 79″ × 80″. The quilt, begun in 1910, contains over 36,000 pieces, each about 1″ × ³⁄₁₆″.

The Quilt That Walked to Golden

Happy campers with a stove and an Album or Odd Fellows quilt.

ber of her lady friends with an old fashioned quilting bee," *The Greeley Tribune* reported on March 9, 1893. "Ten pairs of deft hands aided the hostess in evolving a pattern that would have gained the approval of a Puritan matron and on the conclusion of the labor the mystic eleven sat down to a table loaded with good things gotten up for the comfort of the inner woman."[25]

Detail from Quilt of Many Colors.

The inner woman was being fulfilled throughout Colorado. "Quilt-making was a social event that my mother looked forward to with pleasure," recalled Hazel Dalziel, whose family lived near Longmont. "All the women took great pride in their quilts which were used for bedspreads, sort of Sunday bedspreads. A quilting bee gave women a chance to get together in the home of one of the group and talk, perhaps to gossip. It

Bedroom of the 1874 Benjamin Prosser Thomas house in Central City.

was a friendly and relaxed atmosphere, and the women were making something of which they were proud. It was a vacation from the long workdays."[26]

In the early years of the twentieth century, members of The Daughters of St. John, an Episcopalian club for ladies in Breckenridge, met regularly to sew, while one member read aloud from some uplifting work. One evening in 1912, the women gathered at the home of Mabel Gore, whose husband was dredge master on the Reliance Dredge, one of the gold boats that ripped up the streams of Summit County in search of gold. When there was a knock on the door, Mabel's daughter, Zoe, answered it, thinking her father had come home. Instead, a drunken man rushed into the parlor and grabbed her, saying, "I'll take you, Katie." When her daughter screamed, Mabel Gore, who was barely five feet tall, grabbed a copy of the *Delineator*, a fashion magazine, and, as her terrified guests clutched their sewing, Mabel beat off the man, shoving him out into the street. Later, Mabel found out that the drunk had asked a local man for directions to the "whorehouse." But the stranger had slurred his words so badly that he was misunderstood and directed to the "Gore house" instead.[27]

Most sewing bees were more sedate. "Mrs. Roswell is making a pretty quilt. It is called the flower garden. It is cut out blocks in hexigon shape sewed in circles. She says the ladies down there have gotten up a club and they want all the Buckhorn ladies to attend. They only meet once a month and it is not a dress up club. They are to come in their house dresses," Stella Dickerson in Eggers wrote to her daughter in 1932.[28]

Sewing bees were not just about sewing and socializing; they were a way to get away from the monotony of rural life. "Thelma & Mo went to the Sewing Circle," Mary Knackstedt Dyck recorded in her diary on April 1, 1937. Mary, who lived in Hamilton County, Kansas, wrote about dust storms and radio programs and picture shows, such as "Love is News" starring Don Ameche, and she made frequent references to quilting—cutting out pieces for "Dimondfield," "Wayes" of the World, Flower Garden, and Tulip quilts. "Mo went to the quilting party to Mrs. Bishop." (April 15, 1937.) "Ma ironed another batch of quilt pieces this A.M. and tor apart the small charm quilt." (June 9, 1938.) "I went to Bishops at 1 P.M. to help quilt." (December 1, 1938.) "Iva invited us to come & help her

quilt." (April 7, 1939.) "Pop & Cliff took me to the Hall to help the wimen quilt on eldas quilt." (October 12, 1939.) "Us wimen finished up the apricue [applique] quilt. I was there 3⅔ hour." (October 3, 1940.)[29]

Many sewing circles were formal, with roll call, a club song, and a proper name. The Jolly Stitchers Club, the Recovery Club, and the Helping Hand Club all operated in the Springfield area. The Jolly Thimble Club met in Grand Junction, the Ladies Sewing Circle in Burlington, and the Ladies Aid Society in Keota.[30]

Most of the sewing bees were held among rural women, since, as the century wore on, city ladies often found quilts unfashionable, preferring store-bought spreads or, if they couldn't afford to purchase bedding, turning their quilts upside down so that the whole-cloth backing showed. "City ladies wouldn't have quilts, but country ladies weren't influenced by city ideas," said quilt historian Jeananne Wright. "Farm women were always the mainstay of quilting."[31]

Nonetheless, there were some city sewing circles. In the 1930s, Jennie Toothaker and her daughter, Bessie Toothacker Hickey, held sewing bees in the third floor of their house, which was adjacent to the Toothaker Greenhouse at 448 Josephine in Denver. They invited other women, probably friends and neighbors, to join them in the attic room, where a quilt frame was always set up.[32] And Denver alumnae of Pi Beta Phi,

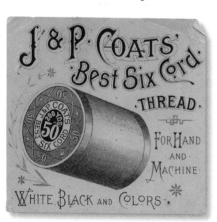

a college sorority, met regularly to quilt, recalled Alberta Iliff Shattuck, a Pi Phi and step-grand-daughter of Elizabeth Sarah Fraser, the sewing machine saleswoman.[33]

Women in Two Buttes organized the Jolly Stitchers Club in 1932. Members pieced and quilted quilts and embroidered tea towels. They made friendship quilts for each other and "came up with some unique designs as well as the old favorites such as the double wedding Ring, wild goose pattern, dresden plate, drunkard's path and lots more.

Pennant Quilt, c. 1920, maker unknown. Wool felt, velveteens, satins, and cottons, foundation-pieced by hand and hand-embroidered, 63″ × 86″. The pennants, mostly from Colorado, California, Arizona, Connecticut, and Oregon, probably were purchased as souvenirs.

Mable Leffler Connor, second row, right, and friends Hazel, Mildred, and Harriott Bush, near Hereford. Mable's mother kept sewing baskets next to her favorite chairs so that she could piece quilt blocks whenever she sat down. Background quilt is Ocean Waves.

The drunkard's path could be put together in several ways to make different designs," remembered Jessie Scobee, a club member.

"I would like to give you some idea what the Jolly Stitchers meant to us during the terrible drought days of the '30s. We had very little money for recreation so we did the best to make things pleasurable for us and our families," she continued. On club day, the members brought their families. While the women cooked and quilted, the men played cards, and the children engaged in games. "I really don't know what we would have done without our club and the friendship and love we had for each other in those hard times we all had to go through together," Jessie said.[34]

Many women turned to sewing clubs for support and friendship during the difficult days of the Depression. Harriett and Forrest Dallas had been married only a few weeks

A Log Cabin comes to an ignoble end in an auto camp in Denver. The newspaper headline reads "Wilson Gives All His Time to Battle High Living Cost."

when both lost their jobs at a Kresge's dime store in Moline, Illinois. They moved to his parents' farm in Harveyville, Kansas, in May, 1933. In her journal, Harriett recorded the search for employment, homesickness, adjustment to farm life, and her pleasure in attending a sewing circle with her mother-in-law, Faye Dallas. "Went to Club with Mom today. Sewed—gossiped, & ate everything, nuf for two men," she wrote on May 17, 1933. "Went to Club with Mom—helped quilt. They are all good women. . . ." (June 8, 1933.) "Club tomorrow—something to look forward to a little." (August 9, 1933.) "All of us, including men, at Earharts for Club. We quilted & sewed." (August 10, 1933.) "Put my quilt in frames & started to quilt. It is just so pretty." (August 23, 1933)[35] That quilt, probably the only one she ever made, was a Double Wedding Ring, with pink and green squares where the circles intersected.

The sewing circles not only helped their members, they helped the less fortunate of their communities. In 1936, Ila Lingelbach and other women formed a sewing club in Hereford, Colorado, to help each other quilt, sew carpet rags, and mend. When they learned about a needy sick woman with several children, they immediately set to work making clothes for the family. With their needles, they continued to help others until the club disbanded in 1989.[36] Grace Snyder's sewing club in the Sand Hills of Nebraska made quilts for a family whose clothing and bedding had been blown away by a tornado. Grace was to become Nebraska's best-known quilter. Among her quilts, often pieced as she sat in the car while her husband did farm work, were a Mosaic Hexagon made with 50,000 dime-size pieces and an 87,789-piece Basket Petit

The names and grades of school children are embroidered on the Sunbonnet Sue quilt.

Ohio Rose, 1930, made by Mattie Jones, Neb. Cottons, hand- and machine-pieced, hand-appliquéd, and hand-quilted, 86" × 88".

The Quilt That Walked to Golden

Point.[37] Other women made quilts that were raffled off to raise money for good causes. Methodist women in Keota embroidered names of Keota and New Raymer homesteaders on a quilt, charging twenty-five cents each for the honor. They spent months embroidering the names and red roses, and when the quilt was finished, its winner's name was drawn from a hat. The ladies made about twenty dollars for their labor.[38]

Most of the recipients of such needlework generosity were grateful, but not all. In "Goose Pasture," a poem about a poor young mother in Summit County, Breckenridge poet Belle Turnbull wrote:

Eula Castleman Miles, member of a northwest Colorado pioneer family, Christmas, 1930. A crazy quilt covers her lap. The Churn Dash quilt top on the floor was never quilted.

> *So the Ladies of Star wheeled out their banners,*
> *Whipped a layette to a froth and lugged it*
> *Through snowbanks shifting down the pasture.*
> *She met them queenly in her manners*
> *Said: Please be seated on the bed.*
> *Said: Oh I'm sure you mean so kind.*
> *But there wasn't a scrap she would take of those ladies,*
> *Not so much as a piece of raveling-thread.*[39]

Colorado ladies remembered the not-so-needy with their needles, too. "Sometime along here Alice Roosevelt is to be married. We felt very near to her. You see, this was Romance, and having none of our own we took part of hers," wrote Anne Ellis. "All the country was sending her gifts, so we, not to be outdone, decided to send one also. . . .We thought of a quilt, each woman doing a certain amount of work on it." But the women decided a quilt was not dainty enough, so one woman made a centerpiece of Battenberg lace, the others paying her fifty cents each. When the lace was finished, Anne herself wrapped it and sent it off, waiting anxiously for a reply. "We never heard a word," Anne wrote. "Alice, how could you?"[40]

Spring cleaning.

Quilts in War and Peace

As the Depression gave way, many women turned their needles to the war effort, just as they had done in previous wars. During World War I, for instance, a pioneer Nebraska woman recorded in her diary, "Minnie come down here for dinner so she helped Nette wash dishes . . . then in a little bit they got ready to go to Red Cross . . . they tied a comforter."[41]

The Red Cross was the center of many women's efforts during World War II. "We did work for the Red Cross, such as knitting Army and Navy sweaters, sewing shirts and rolling bandages out of old sheets and pillow cases," said Jessie Scobee of the Jolly Stitchers Club in Two Buttes.[42] The Navy mothers in Clear Creek County were ordered to make ten Marine Watch quilts, in a pattern as regimented as the service itself. Each quilt was to be 72″ × 84″, made of six-inch squares cut from used wool clothing. The Clear Creek *Mining Journal* noted that the Navy Mothers would meet at the Elks Club to make arrangements for the quilts and were asking local people to donate clothing to be cut up for squares.[43]

Women also made patriotic quilts, piecing flags and appliquéing eagles and stars. Popular in the nineteenth century, commemorative quilts made a comeback during World War II, marking specific events. Ida Johnson Beattie of Denver spent the long years of the war working on a quilt to memorialize her son, Irving, who was captured by the Japanese. Irving survived the Bataan Death March and more than three years of brutal imprisonment, part of it in a leper colony, to return home at the war's end.[44] In Nebraska, Grace Snyder's Helping Hand Club, whose members ranged from the rancher's wife to the hired man's wife, "exchanged their quilting needles for knitting needles and began turning out sweaters, socks, and wash cloths by the bale." The members also held Red Cross benefit dances, including a barn dance and oyster supper, to raise money for the war effort.[45] Many women put down their needles altogether during World War II because they went to work in defense fac-tories or took over men's jobs while the men were at war. Some women, of course, joined the armed services themselves.

At war's end, when thousands of veterans and their wives and others moved to Colorado to start new lives, the women once more picked up their needles as a way to make friends. In 1948, Marie Overdier, who had learned to sew as a little girl, sitting underneath a quilt frame while her aunts quilted, moved from Iowa to a trailer camp in north Denver. During the time she lived there, she quilted with her new neighbors. "You get acquainted with many people," recalled Marie, who began sewing by making doll clothes and quilts and made her first full-size quilt at age sixteen. When she was married in 1936, she received a used treadle sewing machine that cost fifteen dollars. Her favorite pattern was Grandmother's Flower Garden. "I saw a woman who made one with pieces the size of a dime," she said.[46]

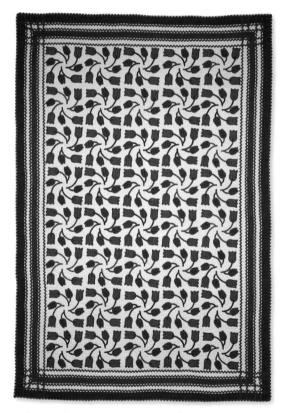

Tulip Swirl, c. 1925–1950, maker unknown. Cottons, machine-pieced, hand-appliquéd, hand-embroidered, and hand-quilted, 68″ × 98¾″. This may have been made from a kit.

Scrap Quilt, c. 1950, made by the Gardiner sisters, Crested Butte, Colo. Cottons, hand- and machine-pieced and hand-quilted, 78″ × 91″. Several Gardiner sisters lived in Crested Butte, where they spent their evenings sitting around a quilt frame, working together.

A Community of Extraordinary Quilters

The first half of the twentieth century produced "name" quilters, women whose quilts were marked by imagination, extraordinary execution, or sheer size of output. Their work today is prized by private collectors and displayed in museums not just in Colorado, but across the country. Among them was Charlotte Jane Whitehill, who began serious quilting in 1929 at age 63. Whitehill, a widow who worked for an insurance company in Emporia, Kansas, was part of a community of extraordinary quilters that included Rose Good Kretsinger, nationally known for her writing, her quilts, and her quilt designs. Charlotte undoubtedly was inspired by Rose, although she probably had learned quilting as a girl from her mother. Her quilts, most of them appliqué, are copies of family and museum quilts. About 1940, Charlotte moved to Denver, and in 1955, she donated thirty-five quilts (six made by her mother, the rest by Charlotte) to the Denver Art Museum. They formed the basis of the museum's textile collection.[47]

While Charlotte Whitehill produced show quilts, other well-known Colorado quilters turned out utilitarian quilts, made not for display but to be used. Among them were the women today known as the Keota Quilters, a pocket of farm women in northeastern Colorado, near the town of Keota. They are "significant because we want a quilting heritage," said Jeananne Wright. "We can see it shining through their collections."[48] These women used old patterns, but they made up their own, as well—whimsical designs such as coffee cups and pumps and houses. Quilt purists who preferred traditional quilts—the Baltimore Albums and Center Medallions that were popular in the mid-nineteenth century in the East, for instance—were horrified at the new realistic designs. Quilt historian Ruth E. Finley ranted about an era that gave children nicknames ending in "y" or "ie," replaced handwork with the sewing machine, designed "gimcrack houses called 'Queen Anne,'" and made quilts such as The Old Town Pump that "were grotesque in the extreme."[49] Colorado quilters paid her no mind and made what they liked.

Mary Stanley was one of those folk artists. She nearly didn't live long enough to become a notable quilter. Told she would die in six months from tuberculosis, Mary, along with her husband, Daniel, and their children, moved to Colorado from Missouri in 1898, hoping to restore her health. The change of locale worked, and after

Auriel Stanstead and Jeananne Wright with a Weathervane
Album in front of the house at Sunshine Corner.

Keota Quilt Retreat

The rain was pouring down in Keota,
but fifteen women drove down the
muddy country road to crowd into
the weathered yellow house at Sunshine
Corner. They were quilters mostly, come
with their covered dishes and their folded
quilts to share stories, show their treasures,
and take a few stitches in the Double Ax
Head set up in a frame in the parlor. The
frame was the first one Clarence Evans
made for his wife, Lula, many years before.
It had passed on to Auriel Oram Sandstead,
whose grandmother, the Keota quilter Mary
Stanley, once lived in the yellow house. In
fact, in the 1970s, when the house was
boarded up, a thief broke in and stole a
steamer trunk and a cedar chest filled with
her quilts.

Not all of Mary's work was taken,
however. She had pieced the Double Ax
Head top that was on the frame, gave it her

own touch, as quilters do, by making each
ax head out of two different fabrics instead
of one, piecing the halves down the middle.
The women who came to the Keota Quilt
Retreat had stitched on the quilt for three
summers, "coming up four," said Auriel.

The retreat draws visitors from all over
Colorado and from Iowa, Nebraska,
Wyoming, Kansas, and other parts of the
country. It began in 1977 with a show of
some fifty quilts, rugs, samplers, and
embroideries. Since 1982, it has been held
twice each summer, three days in June and
another three in August. "Like a streetcar, if
you miss one, another comes along," said
Auriel. Most of those who come along are
women, but there are men, too, and a few
children. Some have ties to Keota. Quilt
historian Jeananne Wright grew up on a
ranch not far away; her grandfather
homesteaded in Keota in 1910. "My
grandmother stood up to quilt," Jeananne
told Auriel, as the two sat beside each other
at the corner of the quilt frame.

"My grandmother sat on that stool over
there. She put her feet on the bottom rung,"
Auriel replied. "That made her arm high
enough to quilt."

The visiting quilters swell the number
of people in this little town, which is set on
the green prairie in the northeast corner
of Colorado. In 1915, the farming and
ranching community had 500 registered
voters, but now there are just three
households in Keota, plus Auriel, who
comes each summer. "When I'm not here, it
makes a twenty-five percent difference," she
joked. Only a handful of boarded-up

buildings, such as the brick Farmers and Merchants Building across the street, remain. Auriel's house, built about 1920 by the town doctor, showed its age, but the three rooms on the first floor (another two up) were cheerful. In the kitchen, hot water for tea boiled on the iron cookstove. A Coors Malted Milk container and other antique food tins were propped up on the spindly-legged ice box. Jadite dishes were stacked in a cupboard. Glass bottles decorated the window—amber bottles in one, green in another. On a painted kitchen table was a vase of field flowers; a jar of Queen Anne's Lace stood in a corner.

The quilt frame, surrounded by mismatched kitchen chairs, dominated the parlor, as it must have in Mary's day. Quilts from Auriel's Keota Quilt Collection were everywhere—a Weathervane Album, a Keota Cactus, a doll quilt made from 1930s fabrics, a quilted triangle in red, white, and blue, made as a memorial to Auriel's grandfather. Pictures of quilts were pinned to the wall, along with snapshots and old photographs from Keota's heyday.

There is no registration, no charge, you simply show up and are welcomed as an old friend, given a square of calico and one of Auriel's chatty letters. She serves as the historian of Keota and keeper of the flame for the Keota quilters.

Visitors on that early June day, when the damp prairie was bright with flowers, admired the Double Ax Head and showed off the quilts they had brought, remarking on the tiny stitches and the fabrics. One woman pointed to a paisley, calling it "Persian Pickle." They talked about the old days in Keota, about quilting—and

about politics and the news. Like the Keota quilters of another generation, the visitors at the Keota quilting bee are interested in more than nostalgia. They gather for many reasons.

One is fellowship. "I love the ladies, love to talk to them. I always come down and visit," said Betty Bivens, who moved to Keota in 1957. She doesn't quilt. "My stitches look like a horse galloping," she laughed. She remembered the Jolly Neighbors, a sewing club in the area, where she was told, "Don't put a knot in the thread, and if we don't like it, we'll just pull it through." Most of those who go to Keota—they include Pat Hubbard, a professional quilter; Shirley Sanden, a quilt teacher; Janet Finley, former director of the Rocky Mountain Quilt Museum; and years ago, Eugenia Mitchell, who founded the museum—are comfortable knotting the thread, however.

As the rain let up, the women hurried to their cars for the drive home, through green prairie grass where they caught glimpses of antelope; it is two hours to Denver, half the drive on a country road, half on the Interstate. Auriel was left behind to pick up the paper plates and wash the forks, then ready her grandmother's house for the next day's quilters. She didn't mind. The quilt retreat is Keota's biggest event, she said, and "it keeps the prairie bubblin'."[1]

Auriel Orem Sandstead stitches on the Double Ax Head.

[1] Sandra Dallas, interviews, Keota, June 5, 2003.

living long enough in Boulder to prove Mary's doctor wrong, Mary and Dan filed for a homestead at Hightower, north of Greeley, in 1910. They lived in a rock house on what they called Hightower Homestead until his death in 1945. After that, Mary divided her time between the homestead and a house in Keota. She died in 1955, at age eighty-five.

During those years on the prairie, Mary stitched in the light that flowed through curtains she had crocheted from grocery twine or under the glare of a kerosene lamp. Prior to her marriage, Mary had been apprenticed to a dressmaker, and she continued "to sew for most anyone," said her granddaughter Auriel Oram Sandstead, quilter and author. Mary had a sewing machine, and "before Simplicity patterns, she used a dressmaker's drafting machine," Auriel added. The machine was essentially a collection of brass slats that Mary laid out on a table to conform to a customer's measurements. As a result of her life-long dressmaking, Mary "had lots of scraps in her scrap bag," Auriel said. So she made mostly scrap-bag quilts, pieced from fabric left over from dresses and shirts that she had made. Mary traded scraps with friends and utilized country fair ribbons in her quilts. She bleached flour and sugar sacks and colored them with Rit dyes or a homemade dye produced by soaking crepe paper in a mason jar with hot water, then using salt to fix the dye.

Mary's patterns were typical of those used by prairie women, and she was quick to pick up popular designs. She produced a blue-and-white Ohio Star in 1913, friendship quilts for her daughter and daughter-in-law, an appliquéd Colonial Girl in the 1930s, and a Trip Around the World in 1940. She frequently edged her quilts with Prairie Points (folded triangles of fabric) and, in fact, is responsible for adding that term to quilting lingo.

Mary was the matriarch of four generations of quilters, but her influence today goes beyond her family. She is, in part, responsible for Colorado's quilt revival since she inspired her granddaughter Auriel to organize an annual quilt retreat in Keota, Colorado. It began in 1977 with a show of Mary's quilts and is now an annual event. (Keota was a favorite site of author James Michener when he wrote his epic Colorado novel, *Centennial*, published in 1974. The book is dedicated to three men, one of them Clyde Stanley, Mary's son.)[50]

Keota quilter Mary Stanley pieces a quilt square in 1913.

"Joy, Happiness and Contentment"

Among the most prolific of the prairie scrap quilters was Lula Reineka Evans, whose ranch straddled the Colorado-Nebraska border near Sidney, Nebraska, and whose work spanned nearly a century of quilting on the Great Plains. Some 125 of her quilts are in the Colorado Springs Pioneers Museum, and she made many more that she gave to friends and relatives.

Born in 1899, Lula learned farming from her father by day and quilting from her mother at night. When she was forty-five, Lula married a neighbor, Clarence Evans, and the couple lived on Lula's property, where they farmed, and Lula made quilts. Her quilts are a rich array of fabrics, patterns, and techniques, embracing the fads and fashions of her lifetime. They run the gamut from a Double Wedding Ring to a Postage Stamp, an ABC Nursery Rhyme to a Tumbling Blocks, a Bicentennial Sampler to a Sunflower. Quilt purist Ruth E. Finley would have hated them.

Using a Mountain Mist pattern, Lula made the Sunflower during a Great Depression dust storm. "I pulled the shades and brought out these materials and started this quilt," she recalled in notes about the Colorado Springs Pioneers Museum collection. "I've always enjoyed making quilts for the joy, pleasure, happiness and contentment they gave me and, to me, the beautiful results."

Lula was an active farm wife, and among her homey belongings were recipes for Black Magic Chocolate Cake, Raisin Quickie Pudding, and Malted Milk Cake. She left behind a book of Tennyson's poems and a little poem about twenty "froggies." But her heart was never far from her quilt scraps. A piece of lace was used for a bookmark in her Bible, and quilt pattern pieces were scattered among her effects.

Lula not only made her own quilts from scratch, but she collected squares and quilt tops

Lula Evans, right, not only pieced her own quilts but bought up quilt squares and tops from others.

Lula Evans with a Dutchman's Puzzle.

that others made, then finished them off. Her advertisements for quilt pieces in several magazines, such as *Farm Wife News* and *Women's Circle*, drew a wide response. "Dear Unknown friend," one letter began. Another woman wrote, "Dear Lady of W.C." A woman in Texas wrote, "I had one large star top finished set together with 3 different colors then I have one 8 point star which needs to be set together. 48 small stars. I would like to have $3.00 a piece for them. I am an old lady 65 years old and live of Social Security am disable to work so this would help me out. . . ." Not long before Lula died in 1993, a friend wrote, "I've wanted to tell you how much you and your quilts have inspired me . . . to see what you have done in your lifetime has sparked a whole new awareness in me."[51]

That awareness was one of the legacies of the scrap quilters of the twentieth century. They kept the craft of quilting alive. They preserved the techniques and patterns of American quilting. And they inspired modern quilters, who no longer are dependent on the scrap bag for their supplies, to embrace quilting methods of the past as well as to create new quilting traditions of their own.

Quilting Again

"Quilting becomes . . . a metaphor for what you do in life."

Judith Trager

Cindy Harp learned to sew when she was three years old. As a young girl, living in rural Missouri, she fashioned her own clothes. Later on, Cindy altered garments for dry cleaners, worked on custom bridal gowns, and made stuffed bunnies for a craft shop. But she didn't quilt. Cindy's great-grandmother had pieced a Grandmother's Flower Garden, but Cindy's mother had no interest in quilting. "She thought it was too hard," Cindy said. Cindy herself had pieced a few Log Cabin blocks when she was eight, in 1966, but they were crooked and made from a hodge-podge of flannel, seersucker, heavy cotton, and cotten blends. She dumped the squares into a drawer, and years later, when she came across them, she didn't even remember making them.

History of Colorado Trains, 1994, made by RMQM volunteers, Golden, Colo. Cotton, machine-pieced, hand-appliquéd, hand-embroidered, and hand-quilted, 68¾" × 92½". Top to bottom, Panel 1: Denver-area light rail, Winter Park ski train, Pikes Peak cog railroad. Panel 2: Durango-Silverton narrow gauge railroad. Panel 3: Ft. Collins trolley, Georgetown Loop. Panel 4: Cumbres & Toltec railroad. Panel 5: Como roundhouse, Moffat Tunnel.

Then, in 1988, while working in a quilt shop, Cindy decided it was time to learn to quilt. Since she was selling patterns and fabric, she thought she ought to know what to do with them. She discovered the childhood quilt squares and figured she'd attempt Log Cabin a second time. But Log Cabin wasn't for Cindy. She got the directions mixed up, and instead of adding pieces in a clockwise fashion, Cindy, who is left handed, added pieces to some of the blocks in the wrong direction. This time, it was Cindy who found the quilt project "too hard," she said. She's never tried another Log Cabin.

But the quilting stuck. Cindy kept at it, making blocks to be exchanged with friends, then producing wall hangings. A few years later, in 1994, she entered her first quilt competition, in Oklahoma City, and won an award of merit. "Sewing, manipulating fabric is what I think of as my spiritual gift," Cindy said. Sewing "is the second thing I do every day"—after drinking a cup of coffee. "If I get cranky, my family tells me to go sew."

Today, Cindy Harp is a professional quilter, whose work is valued at up to $1,200. Her output, mostly wall hangings with subject matter ranging from traditional blocks representing five generations of quilting to a cross on a mosaic of colored scraps, has been shown throughout the country. Cindy lectures and designs quilt patterns. With nine sewing machines—her father found one of them, a hand-operated model with mother-of-pearl inlay, in a chicken coop—she does commercial quilting. And she's taught her mother to quilt. "A day without sewing is like a day without sunshine," Cindy said.[1]

Most quilters today would agree. Not many contemporary quilters are as proficient or have taken their quilting quite so far as Cindy Harp has. Still, Cindy is typical of the women who revived quilting in Colorado—and all across America, for that matter—and who dominate the craft today. Taught at least marginal sewing skills as girls, they nonetheless were not raised as quilters. They discovered quilting on their own in the last quarter of the twentieth century and became as devoted to quilting as their grandmothers had been before them. And they introduced a standard of creativity and workmanship never before seen in American quilting. These reborn quilters caused an explosion of quilting subject and style unlike anything ever seen in quilting's past.

Out of Fashion

By the time World War II was over, quilts and quilting were on the decline. Many women who had gotten their first paychecks by holding down wartime defense jobs continued to work and had little time for handicrafts. Housewives flush with post-war affluence thought that quilting, like making your own clothes, was a sign of the frugal years of the Great Depression. These "young moderns," as newlyweds were called then, preferred store-bought bedcovers, which under-

Sunbonnet Sue and Double Wedding Ring.

scored their prosperity. Besides, there was no place in the sleek, unadorned homes pictured in women's magazines of the 1950s and 1960s for clunky quilts with their homey little scraps of color. Women traded in their thrifty mothers' sewing bees for book groups and Tupperware parties. The new feminist movement frowned on time-consuming, mind-numbing household tasks such as cooking, cleaning, and sewing. Women didn't bring their quilt squares to consciousness-raising meetings.

So for a quarter-century or more, quilting was out of fashion. "I remember my grandmother in a rocking chair quilting, always quilting. My mother sewed beautifully, but she never quilted," said Roberta Spillman, who lives in Cedaredge. "I don't remember the subject of quilting ever coming up." Roberta made her first quilt in the mid-1970s, "for the sense of accomplishment" it gave her, she said. Later, her daughter made quilts for competitions.[2]

Of course, there were some women who never gave up quilting. Many of them lived in rural areas where quilting bees continued to be an excuse for

Upside down on King David's Crown.

getting together. The Last Chance Quilters in Last Chance, a prairie crossroads, didn't give a hoot whether quilting was fashionable. The women met regularly, in good times and bad, to quilt and talk and listen to devotional readings, just as they had done since 1926. Over the years, the membership remained steady, at about a dozen. "They kind of feel like a family. It seems like I hate to miss it," said Opal Roderick, who joined in the 1950s.[3]

In Harveyville, Kansas, the United Methodist Quilting Ladies, whose members began meeting at the same time as the Last Chance women, continued their weekly quilting to raise money for the church. "It's the friendship," explained Georga Umberger, in 1992. Then eighty-nine, she nonetheless was still able to take five tiny stitches at a time

Paulette Tilden is surrounded by her grandmother's quilts, in Denver, 1950. They include Double Wedding Ring, Trip Around the World, Colonial Lady, Sunbonnet Sue, and Grandmother's Flower Garden.

on her needle. Georga, who had moved thirty miles away to Topeka by then but made the trip back to Harveyville several times a year to stitch with her friends, was unsure how long she'd attended the quiltings. "My stars, I wouldn't have an idea," she said.

Elma Wilson, Paulette's grandmother, with her treasury of quilts, Denver, 1950.

Another United Methodist quilting lady, Florence Smitha, remarked, "I don't know how many quilts I've made, but I'm ready to quit." "You'll be making another one," her friend Lena Ginter told her.[4] And Lena was right. Nonetheless, for a generation, most women did put down their quilting needles.

Revival

Women did not pick up their needles again until the 1970s, when quilts returned, not only to the bedroom but to the living room, too. In 1971, the Whitney Museum in New York held a show of

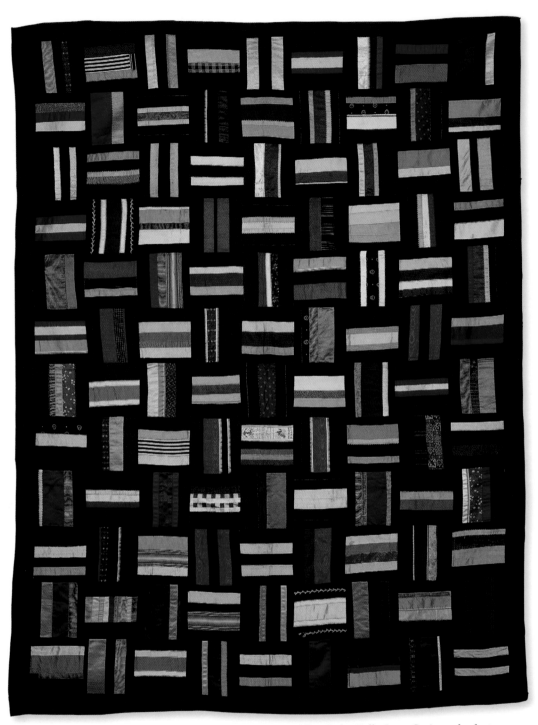

Rail Fence variation, c. 1890, made by Hannah Sturgis Miller, Cedar Falls, Iowa. Satin and velvet ribbons, machine-pieced and hand-finished, 49″ × 63″.

The Quilt That Walked to Golden

The Denver Art Museum's 1974 quilt show encouraged patrons to view quilts as art.

American pieced quilts that had been selected because each worked "as a 'painting,'" wrote Jonathan Holstein, one of the collectors whose quilts were displayed. "Our interest is in the image the quilts form, and not in their stitches."[5] The idea of quilts as art was novel, because until then, quilting had been considered a craft and such an unimportant one that few women signed their work. Only the very finest quilts were saved. The rest were meant to be used up.

The Whitney was not the only museum to discover quilts. In 1974, the Denver Art Museum held an exhibition of quilts and coverlets. The museum had opened a new six-storey facility just two years earlier, with a large textile gallery that featured a permanent display of quilts. The exhibition, held in the museum's main gallery, was made up of more than a third of the 200 quilts and coverlets in the museum's collection. They included quilts that Charlotte Jane Whitehill had donated, along with those that "were given to us a long, long time ago, when the elder generation that supported the museum left things to it," said Imelda DeGraw, who was then Curator of Textiles and Costumes. One of the quilts in the exhibit and one that frequently is on display today is the Matterhorn Quilt, pieced in 1934 by Myrtle M. Fortner, depicting the famed Swiss Peak, with trees and cabins in the foreground. It's not only art, but made entirely of one-inch squares, it's virtually pointillism.

The quilt show, which opened to the sounds of fiddles and a square dance caller, was an outstanding success. "One of the things I marveled at was the number of men, by themselves or with women, and they didn't appear to have been dragged in by the nose," said Imelda. The owner of a downtown Denver cigar store visited the exhibit and told the curator that he had records identifying manufacturers whose names were printed on the bands used in a quilt made of cigar silks that was on display. "Give me the quilt, and I'll find out all those companies that made the cigars," he told her. Imelda replied, "I'm not giving it to you. You'll have to bring those books here."[6]

Quilting eventually received a boost from feminists, who dubbed quilts, samplers, and hand-hooked rugs "women's art." "The women's movement strove to elicit value for items made by women and gave us a new way of thinking about our mothers," said Shirley Sanden, a quilt instructor in Wheat Ridge.[7] Quilt shows "validated and honored women's work," added Cindy Harp.[8]

About the time of the Whitney show, the Mountain Artisans, a West Virginia quilt cooperative, was formed as part of that state's war on poverty. The artisans' colorful quilts, as well as pieced and appliquéd clothing, became a hit with major department stores, such as Neiman Marcus, and drew the attention of *Vogue*, *The New York Times*, and publications all across the country. The artisans' designs were so simple and easy to assemble—and many were tacked instead of quilted—that women who'd never quilted before were inspired to copy them. In Colorado, women wearing Mountain Artisans-style denim skirts with machine-appliquéd flowers made their first quilts by tackling the Appalachian patterns.[9]

But the greatest reason for a revival of quilting undoubtedly was America's 1976 Bicentennial (and Colorado's Centennial) celebration with its emphasis on heritage. Americans rediscovered the homey crafts that once had graced American dwellings. "Quilts had a warm and fuzzy connection to the country's past. There was an association in people's minds between the Bicentennial and quilting," said Bonnie Leman, founder of *Quilter's Newsletter Magazine*.[10] So antique American quilts were hung in museums and stores, offices, hotel lobbies, and public buildings.

Women's Gold

As part of Colorado's Centennial celebration, two Georgetown women, Eva Mackintosh and Geraldine Merrill, designed a stitchery project honoring women. At first, they thought they might do something in macramé, but macramé was too trendy, so they settled on an embroidered and appliquéd tapestry. They dubbed it "Women's Gold," for the Harison's yellow roses that the pioneer women brought west with them in their covered wagons. The tapestry would commemorate only women because "the story of the women's achievements, courage, loyalty, love of beauty would speak clearly to generations of Americans in the Twenty First Century," wrote Mary Coyle Chase, the Pulitzer Prize-winning author of *Harvey*, in her foreword to *Women's Gold*, a booklet about the tapestry. Besides, she added, the story of men's achievements had been told often enough.

Once the nine-by-twelve-foot tapestry was prepared and the most difficult parts worked by skilled embroiderer Betsy Gottschalk, it was set up in public places such as department stores and high school gymnasiums throughout the state, so that Coloradoans could take stitches in it. Some 3,500 did, from Colorado's first ladies Ann Love and Dottie Lamm to boxer Ron Lyle and football player Roosevelt Greer. They stitched

Dr. Antonia Brico, conductor of the Business Men's Orchestra in Denver, left, watches women stitch on Women's Gold at the Denver Dry Goods. Geraldine Merrill, rear right, was one of the women responsible for the tapestry.

Buffalo Bill, 1996, constructed by four women and quilted by Opal Frey, Arvada, Colo. Cottons, machine- and hand-pieced and hand-quilted, 77″ × 93″. William Cody was a famous scout, hunter, and showman. He died in Denver, where in later years, he was best known for his prodigious drinking.

on nineteen female figures, which included Chase, a Denver resident; Aunt Clara Brown, a former slave who became a Central City washerwoman; and Margaret Crawford, who used her precious drinking water to nourish the Harison' rose starts she brought with her on the Overland Trail. While the wall hanging was a tapestry, not a quilt, it nonetheless emphasized stitchery as women's art and encouraged women to pursue the various needle arts. In 1977, it was hung permanently in the state capitol building in Denver.[11]

Slightly more than a decade later, the Colorado Quilting Council (CQC) sponsored a quilt show in the state capitol with some 200 quilts, all with a connection to Colorado, hung throughout the building. "We had a hard time getting into the capitol," remembered Opal Frey, a CQC member and curator at the Rocky Mountain Quilt Museum. "They told us 'no way.'" But CQC members persisted, and the capitol show was so popular that it has been held every two years since then. Formed in 1978 by twenty-six women, the council, which had grown to 1,400 members in 2003, was a major force in bringing together Colorado quilters and in promoting quilting throughout the state. Besides monthly meetings in locations all over Colorado, CQC holds symposiums and sponsors an annual Quilt-A-Fair, where thousands of quilters and collectors purchase antique and new quilts and quilting paraphernalia.[12]

The interest in newly rediscovered American heritage inspired a country-style decorating trend with an emphasis on folk art. Up until then, Early American décor generally meant elegant highboys and four-poster beds with chintz quilts. Now Americans began looking for simpler antiques—painted farm tables and pie safes, yellow ware bowls and butter paddles, hand-lettered signs and bird houses. And they rediscovered quilts, which could be spread on beds, thrown over sofas and chairs, and now, thanks to shows at the Whitney, the Denver Art Museum, and other institutions, even hung on walls. Collectors snapped up fine quilts in pristine condition, but they also bought calico Nine Patch and scrap quilts that were lovingly aged. They found them in antiques stores and flea markets and by inquiring at farm houses. "People come to the door and say: 'You got any old quilts?'" said Florence Smitha in Harveyville. "Tell me why people's so crazy about old quilts. If I was going to buy a quilt, I wouldn't buy an old one," added Mary Sue Phillips.[13]

"Quilting Is Cool"

Plenty of collectors would and did buy older quilts. Still, while women admired the old quilts, many wanted new ones for their homes, quilts made with their own hands. But this new generation of quilters was different from their mothers and grandmothers, who had relied on their scrap bags for quilt fabric. Economy no longer was the driving force behind their quilting. Neither was making bedcovers. Quilters picked up their needles to express themselves, to create heirlooms, to bring softness to the hard environment of technology and comfort to a stressful world.

Some had learned sewing years before. Others remembered the skills they'd been taught in the high-school home economics classes that all girls were required to take in the 1940s and 1950s. Many taught themselves to quilt or attended classes in schools, retirement homes, and recreation centers. Longtime quilter Shirley Sanden organized her first quilting class, for Camp Fire Girls, in Wheat Ridge in 1974. She went on to teach classes for senior citizens but continued to instruct girls. She taught her granddaughter, Kaila Mills in Aurora, to quilt in 1996, when Kaila was five. "Quilting is cool," said Kaila, which pretty much sums up the way quilters of all ages feel about it.[14]

Many quilters were self-taught, and they were desperate for information. In 1969, Bonnie Leman tapped into that nascent rebirth of quilting when she began publishing *Quilter's Newsletter Magazine* in Wheat Ridge. Pregnant with her seventh child, Leman, a free-lance writer, wanted to create a job where she could work at home with a steadier income than she had earned writing articles. "I thought up the idea of making quilt-pattern templates out of plastic that wouldn't wear out. I called them 'heirloom plastics,'" she said.

She sold the templates by mail order, and one of her customers suggested she send out a letter with them telling about quilting. Quilters were "hungry for patterns, hungry for encouragement, hungry for information. There was a vacuum out there," she said. So Bonnie, who had never made a quilt, created a chatty sixteen-page letter, eight of those pages filled with ads for her own products. Within a few months, she had moved the operation from her kitchen table into the garage and named the publication *Quilter's Newsletter Magazine*. The initial printing was 5,000 copies, which cost her $200. The publication included patterns, stories, a quilt lesson, and a forum for readers' letters called Quilting Bee. "I wanted a news column with information on what was hap-

An Indian woman in Montana works on a quilt top made from men's ties.

pening in quilting," said Bonnie. "Of course, not much was happening then, so this was a short feature." It's much longer today, although the contents of the magazine have changed little in thirty-five years. The print run has grown substantially, to 250,000 copies, with subscribers in all fifty states and 100 foreign countries. Later, Bonnie added a second magazine, *Quiltmaker*, and began a publishing company. She sold her operation in 1991, and it now is owned by Primedia Incorporated.

Bonnie also started a quilt shop, Quilts and Other Comforts, in Arvada, in the early 1970s, and operated it for five years.[15] Many women learned to quilt there and at Quilts in the Attic, which opened in 1975 in a tiny second-floor space in Old South Gaylord, an historic shopping area in Denver. It later expanded to fill the entire building. Two women lunching across the street discovered the vacant space and leased it. "We did needlepoint, but there was already a needlepoint shop on the block. So we opened a quilt shop," said Marge Hedges. She was one of four partners, each of whom put up $2,000 to start Quilts in the Attic. The women stocked it with 100 percent cotton fabric, which was not easy to find in those days, and quilting supplies, including batting, patterns, quilting thread, and hoops. "We thought every stitch had to be done by hand. But we decided otherwise. If it took a woman a year to make a quilt by hand, we weren't going to have much business," Marge recalled.

Blocks and Pinwheels.

The day the shop opened, a woman telephoned to ask if anyone could show her how to make a Cathedral Window quilt. The clerk who answered the phone assured her she could, then hung up and asked, "Quick, do we have a book that shows how to make one?" Marge remembered. By the time the customer arrived, the women had found the pattern.

Carol Goin, left, and Sally Pape pin-baste Carol's Fifty-four Forty or Fight or Tennessee Waltz at a retreat at the Blue Jay Inn, Buffalo Creek, in 1989.

The four women originally had thought the shop might stay in business for a few years, until women grew tired of quilting. But quilters came in droves and still do, sometimes by the busload from eastern Colorado, just to buy fabric. Others made trips from neighboring states. "They buy the fabric without anything in mind. They buy it because it's gorgeous. It's like a feeding frenzy," Marge said. She estimated the average quilter who came into her store had close to $5,000 worth of fabric squirreled away at home.

For Quilts in the Attic and other quilt shops that sprang up, classes became a vital part of

The Quilt That Walked to Golden

their business and an important part of quilt culture, a commercial way of replacing sewing bees once held in homes. "We became the 'Cheers' of the quilt business," said Marge, who ran the shop for nearly twenty-five years before selling her interest. "We knew everybody's name. We had everyone from the socially prominent to young mothers, every economic situation. If you get them all in a class, they became great friends. Women who quilt are sharing. It's not only the making of the quilt that matters. It's the association with other women, just as it always was. They did it for warmth then. Now they do it for the warmth of the soul."[16]

New Generation of Quilters

The quilters who emerged after Colorado's mid-century quilt hiatus, for the most part, were consistently better quilters than their mothers and grandmothers. "For 200 years, women were busy grubbing out a living. Now they have more time. Today, women have more education in the arts," said Marge Hedges. Besides, "today's quilter has better tools, prettier fabrics, good lights, wonderful sewing machines, rulers, rotary cutters. And they have better teachers. Pioneer women would have been just as creative, but they didn't have the opportunity."[17]

Road Blocks, 1992, made by Patty Hawkins, Estes Park, Colo. Cottons, machine-pieced and machine-quilted, 66" × 77". Patty, one of the country's best known art quilters, based her design on Tumbling Blocks.

Quilting had always been an egalitarian pursuit, with both rich and poor of all ages bent over the hoops and quilting frames. But quilters in the past had been mostly white females. White women returned to quilting, of course, but they were joined by Asians, Hispanics, and African Americans, and by men. In the beginning, "men were hiding in the closet. They were afraid they wouldn't be accepted because they were doing 'women's work,'" said Opal Frey, who organized the Rocky Mountain Quilt Museum's first all-male show in 1993. It became a biennial event.

Internationally known showman Ricky Tims combines music with quilts.

"People expect men's quilts to be different, but they really aren't. Looking at the exhibit, you wouldn't know they're made by men unless somebody told you," Opal said, then added, "they're less flowery."[18] Fewer hearts and teddy bears, too.

"Men tend to like the math part of it, the geometrics of it, the precision design, the drafting," said Janet Finley, former museum director. "They're very serious. They tend to make a business out of it."[19] "If a man goes into quilting, he doesn't do it to hang out with the ladies," agreed Marge Hedges.[20]

One who made a business out of it—and is very comfortable with the ladies—is Ricky Tims, who admonished, "Keep the gender issue out of it. It has nothing to do with my skill to design and create. I'm not out to be a male quilter. I'm just a quilter who happens to be male."

In 1991, Ricky, then a free-lance music producer born in Texas, inherited his grandmother's Kenmore sewing machine and decided to make a western shirt. He soon found the shirt too daunting, so when he came across a book with a picture of a sampler quilt, he thought, "I can make a quilt because it's flat." He cut templates from a cardboard cereal box and drew around them on the quilt with a ballpoint pen. He paid little attention to the instructions for quarter-inch seams, and as a result, the finished blocks, which were supposed to be twelve inches square, varied from eleven to thirteen inches. That didn't faze Ricky. He joined a quilt group, then attended a lecture by nationally known quilter Faye Anderson, who spoke on how the elements of design applied to quilting. "I thought that's exactly what I do in music. I never knew the parallel between art and music," Ricky said. Within a year, he sold his first quilt for $350, a quilt that shortly afterward was appraised at $3,500. In 1998, Ricky quit his job as a church music director in St. Louis to become a full-time quilter, moving to Arvada, Colorado, in 2000.

Ricky produces what he calls traditional quilts with a twist, creating each design, dyeing the fabric, piecing or appliquéing, quilting, and even making the sleeve. Still "making quilts is not my livelihood," he said. He combines the quilts with lecturing, teaching, writing books, and performing, traveling up to twenty-three days each month in the United States and abroad. Each year, he gives about forty multimedia shows, in which his quilts become a backdrop for musical performances. Quilters flock to his programs and to the classes at his studio. In the future, he expects to offer quilt retreats at his forty-acre ranch near LaVeta, Colorado, which he purchased in 2002.

Quilting, he said, "was in the cards. I didn't even think about it. I fell in love with the tactile quality of the fabric, the design potential, the methods of construction. I can't imagine not being a quilt-maker now. It's such a huge part of what I am." And, having won dozens of awards, including a first place at the International Quilt Festival in Houston and another first place at the Museum of the American Quilter's Society in Paducah, he is a huge part of what American quilting is.[21]

Ricky also serves as inspiration for other quilters, both male and female. One is David Taylor, a graphic artist in Steamboat Springs. David didn't start quilting until 1999, when a friend asked him to design a quilt for her to stitch. He'd tried to make a quilt twenty years earlier but "couldn't see how anyone would want to sew those little squares. I didn't know you could create art out of it," he said. After that first quilt sold for $25,000 at a music festival fund-raiser, "I thought that's my art, and somebody wanted to buy it," David said. So he designed a second quilt, which he made himself. It sold, too, and David was on his way. Now, he makes appliquéd and machine-stitched pictorial quilts, generally landscapes with animals, trees, and flowers, and he sells everything he makes.[22]

Many people who were first attracted by the quilt revival of the 1970s were unrestrained by quilting tradition, and as a result, their first efforts were, well, less than successful by today's standards. Hippies in Boulder fashioned quilts out of patches cut from cheap cotton spreads imported from India. The finished work smelled faintly of incense and marijuana. A Denver woman's first attempt at a stuffed quilt, a wedding gift for her sister, produced a bedcover that weighed twenty-five pounds. Hundreds of quilts combined scraps cut from wool, cotton, and synthetic fabrics, something no self-respecting quilter would do today. And then there were double-knits. In 2003, the Rocky Mountain Quilt Museum accepted a Double Ax Head quilt made entirely from double-knits. It had been purchased at a yard sale for less than two dollars. When the quilt was unfolded, members of the museum's Collection Committee were aghast. But when they stopped laughing, they admitted that double-knits, after all, were part of Colorado's quilt history. And perhaps quilt historians 150 years from now would be as excited about studying a rare double-knit quilt (for surely, few of those have been kept as heirlooms) as today's enthusiasts were about finding a Center Medallion or a Baltimore Album. Perhaps.

Such missteps were part of the learning process, and before long, the new quilters began producing a rich variety of quilts. Many quilters in this new generation embraced traditional patterns, utilizing reproduction fabrics, the rich browns and double-pinks and bright calicos of a century earlier. Others turned to contemporary materials to make quilts of their own designs. In the mid-1970s, Libbie Gottschalk began using clothing labels to patch holes in the family quilt that she had rescued from a ragbag. She was not a quilter, but her mother, Betsy, an embroiderer, had worked on the Women's Gold tapestry and passed her love of textiles on to Libbie. The quilt, used for years by Libbie's grandfather in a log cabin on West Chicago Creek near Idaho Springs, had been made of flimsy fabrics and was fragile with age. As the material deteriorated, Libbie added more and more labels, choosing those from Denver retailers such as Neusteter Company, Gano-Downs Company, Denver Dry Goods Company, and Daniels & Fisher Stores Company. But the rips got ahead of her, and before long, Libbie was scrambling for any labels she could find. She shopped garage sales. Friends went through their closets, snipping tags from dresses and coats and even hats. Libbie's sister, Julie Scott, brought back labels from travels to India and Hong Kong.

Over the years, Libbie patched the quilt with labels from upscale designers and foreign manufacturers, chain stores and discount houses. The quilt contained hundreds, possibly thousands, of labels by the time the entire surface was covered in 2003. But that wasn't the end of Libbie's work on the label quilt. Because she used the quilt as a bed cover during the thirty years she worked on it, some of the patches themselves have worn out. Now she uses labels to mend labels.[23]

Women made quilts for their families and friends, and like their grandmothers, they turned sewing into a sort of community outreach program, often through the dozens of quilt guilds that sprang up. High Plains Heritage Quilters in Haxtun, for instance, makes receiving blankets for every newborn in Phillips County and has fashioned quilts for underprivileged children and AIDS and drug patients.

Libbie Gottschalk spent thirty years covering a quilt with hundreds of clothing labels.

Some quilters became pictorial artists. Pat Hubbard, whose great-grandmother, Emily Wilson, had been a pioneer quilter on the Colorado prairie, drew on her own ranching heritage to produce appliquéd quilts with figures of cowboys and pioneers. She had learned sewing from Emily, who often set Pat to work plucking seeds out of her batting. In 1984, while living in Arizona, Pat designed and executed a quilt of desert animals and cactus for a community center fund raiser. She liked the idea of designing figurative quilts, and she went on to make a Kachina Doll quilt. She researched the hand-carved Hopi figures at trading posts and Indian markets. "I had Hopi kids tell me the colors. The adults wouldn't," she said.

In 1989, after returning to northeastern Colorado, Pat designed South Fork of the Oregon Trail, a pictorial quilt made up of hand-drawn and painted pioneers with cov-

South Fork of the Oregon Trail, 1995, made by Pat Hubbard, Greeley, Colo. Cottons, cotton blends, corduroys, and velveteens; hand-appliquéd, hand-embroidered, and hand-quilted, 77″ × 95″. The quilt shows Pat's family migrating west and the Sioux Indians who killed her great-grandfather.

ered wagons and Indians hunting buffalo and sitting in front of tepees. The quilt told the story of Pat's ancestors' westward journey. A similar quilt, Heaven's Eternal Campfire, depicts in appliqué cowboy scenes on earth and in heaven, inspired by her family's ranching days. "When I start creating a story quilt, they're like my children," said Pat, who spends about a year on each quilt. "I 'borned' it. I created it. It's a part of me, and it's a part of my life that's on that fabric." Pat's figures are hand-stitched with nine stitches to the inch, so many that she's been accused of using a sewing machine. But she doesn't "because there's not much love on a machine." She added, "I don't know of anything I don't like about quilting."[24]

As quilts moved into the mainstream again, artists discovered the medium, and they created an entirely new art form—the art quilt. Such quilts generally are smaller than bed quilts and made to be hung on a wall. They transcend craft and are often abstract, but not always, and they're sold in art galleries, not just in quilt shops. Art quilters sometimes fuse their fabrics together, leave raw edges, and utilize non-fabric materials. Art quilts underscore the fact that quilting today is no longer women's art; it's art. And nobody exemplifies that better than Patty Hawkins, an award-winning art quilter, lecturer, and teacher, and one of the reasons Colorado is a center of the art quilt movement.

Patty had been a watercolor artist for fifteen years when she attended the Smithsonian Institution's Craft Today show at the Denver Art Museum in 1987. She was stunned by contemporary art quilts mounted on the ceiling. "It was as though I was seeing stained glass cathedral windows. I thought this is it," she said. Like women of her generation, Patty had learned to sew as a girl. "I thought everybody could sew, so I never took that to be a talent that was artistic," she said. But then she saw the Craft Today show, and that inspired her to take traditional quilting classes "because you have to learn the language and finishing techniques, for darn sure." Occasionally she uses traditional quilt patterns such as Bear Paw and Drunkard's Path, abstracting the designs and working them with wild combinations of fabrics. More often, she is influenced by her Colorado experience, creating abstract mountain landscapes and Anasazi cliff dwellings, and even the reflections in the glass of urban buildings. Her art quilts, most of them abstracts, range from Aerial Baghdad, a series of black-and-white triangles that seem suspended above three-dimensional stripes of red and yellow, to Aspen Seasons. It is a series of vertical stripes, with pieced black-and-white strips representing the trees.

Judith Trager designed country pillows and aprons before becoming a nationally known art quilter.

Working out of a large Estes Park studio with turquoise doors and a view of the Rocky Mountains, Patty said that color is the major emphasis of her work. She dyes most of her fabrics herself "because you can create things that are so unpredictable. It's just my chocolate cake." Still, "I think using a little drop of commercial fabric is good. It punches up the softness of hand-dyed fabrics," she said. Her palette contains a good deal of yellow, but "I love wild, bright, intense colors," she said. She also incorporates black-and-white material, and "I love doing stripes."

Although she sells some of her art and could sell all of it if she chose to, Patty gives many of her art quilts to friends, museums, and to charitable auctions. She creates because "it gives me great pleasure. It's so joyful to take these fabrics and neighbor them to each other. This deliciousness happens. Thank you, God."[25]

Like Patty, most art quilters are artists first and quilters second. "Tradition is the foundation for what I do. It's the floor of the art. I still make quarter-inch seams and press them a certain way," said Boulder art quilter Judith Trager. "We see quilting as a medium, as a new way to use the palette."

Judith, who described herself as "a professional artist who makes quilts," produces as many as thirty quilts each year, and they sell for between $250 and $300 per square yard. She does mostly commissioned work, which hangs in private collections as well as college campuses, hospitals, offices, and public buildings. The three wall hangings that she made in 2003 for the visitors' center at Red Rocks, a Denver mountain park, are abstractions of the giant rock formations. And her quilt hanging in the United States Embassy in Bosnia, which was commissioned by the State Department, is a series of outstretched arms and hands in bright colors—but not red, because red is the color of blood. Institutions are drawn to art quilts "because they're warm and familiar and comforting. People know textiles. They wear them, they've been into them their whole lives," said Judith. "It may look different, but it's still a quilt. People love to touch quilts. They're irresistible. I love it when someone comes up and touches a quilt because it means they have a personal relationship with me."

Judith grew up with a love of both painting and quilting. "I wanted to make a quilt that looked like a painting and a painting that looked like a quilt," she remembered. She began selling her quilts at art fairs in the 1970s in southern Illinois, where she lived. Then she started her own company, The Patch Works, which employed as many as thirty women on a piecework basis, turning out country quilts and pillows and aprons for the wholesale market. With the country look just getting underway, Judith also designed denim-and-calico clothing and accessories kits sold by *Better Homes and Gardens* magazine.

She continued to quilt, while she and her family moved across the country, all the while working at outside jobs. Finally in 1989, when Judith moved to Boulder, her husband and children told her they expected her to become a full-time artist. She set up a bright studio filled with shelves of fab-

Quilt historian Mary Ann Schmidt, fourth from left, and members of the Colorado Quilting Council document a Triangles quilt in Golden, 2001.

rics, a drafting table, story boards of work in progress, and a sign with "cute" crossed out. Now she produces art quilts that are bold abstractions of the western scene as well as interpretations of contemplative landscapes, and explosions of bright color and pattern that come from her childhood in Mexico. "Quilting becomes your life. The fiber becomes a metaphor for what you do in life," she said.[26]

Both Patty Hawkins and Judith Trager are members of the Front Range Contemporary Quilt Organization. Patty, in fact, was one of six women who founded the group in 1988, after first being under the wing of a hand-weavers guild in Boulder. "I was afraid they

Wa Shonaji

A rtie Johnson proudly held up her
Holiday Wishes quilt, a red, white,
and green Christmas design of trees
and stars and candy canes. "All right,
Artie!" cried a member of the Rocky
Mountain Wa Sonaji Quilt Guild. "That is
gorgeous! You keep going!" called a second
admirer. One after another, the women
displayed their quilts—a yellow-and-blue Rail
Fence, a patriotic Lady Liberty, an
hexagonal Celtic design, an eye-catching
abstract entitled Harmony. Each one drew
an enthusiastic reception, with applause
and shouts of "You go, girl!"

The work and the words of encouragement might have come from the members
of any of Colorado's dozens of quilt groups.
This one just happens to be African
American. Wa Shonaji is Swahili for "people
who sew."

And sew they do. "Boy, do we put out
quilts," said Artie. "And as you can see,
beautiful quilts," added another Wa Shonaji
member. The members meet monthly to
share their quilts, learn about quilting, and
quilt together. They attend special
workshops to make comfort quilts that are
given to newborns, the bereaved, and others
who've experienced trauma. They put
together exhibitions for the Rocky
Mountain Quilt Museum and the Colorado
Quilting Council.

Why an African-American quilt guild?
"We wanted a group that was more
culturally specific," explained Helen
Kearney, the only Wa Shonaji founder who
is still a member. "We've got all kinds of
groups—men, gays, women, Amish, Native
Americans. I don't see anything different
about being African American. The question
is why not an African-American group? Why
not get together?"

Wa Shonaji, was founded in 1994 by five
African American women. In 2003, its
members, whose professions include
educator, housewife, and analytical chemist,
numbered thirty-two. Only two-thirds of the
members are black. "I wanted to learn to
quilt, and a woman said we have a bunch of
women who meet. She didn't say they were
African American," said Pennie Estrada, an
Hispanic member. She liked the idea that
members are encouraged to enjoy, not judge,
each other. And she stayed because of the
friendship and the chance to improve her
quilting skills. Wa Shonaji stresses education. Its motto is "Each One Teach One."

After the business meeting and "Show
and Share," Pennie and other members
stayed behind for a quilt lesson. One of the
group's more experienced quilters, Helen,
passed out packets of African fabric and the
pattern for a Tumbling Heart block—a nine
patch with two curved pieces for the top of
the heart. As the women set up their
portable sewing machines and got out their
rotary cutters, Helen began with basic
instructions. If you want a finished square
that is two inches, she said, you start with a
two-and-a-half-inch square, allowing a
quarter-inch all around for a seam.

Juanita Roper, right, shows Wa Shonaji members the African symbol for "readiness to serve." Members make a different symbol each month, until they have twelve quilt blocks.

She asked Pennie to stitch together two long strips of fabric. "This is how you strip quilt," Helen said. She finger-pressed the seam "to the dark side" and showed the quilters how to cut out the double patches. When she finished explaining the nine patch section of Tumbling Heart, Helen tackled the rounded tops of the heart. For curved piecing, she explained, anchor the fabrics at three points, then stitch by hand before sewing on the machine. "Write this down: Sew before snipping," she said.

While Wa Shonaji operates like any other quilt group, it is, after all, an African-

American guild, and its members are charged with preserving their traditions and culture. So the members sometimes draw on their heritage for quilt designs. The guild puts together shows for black museums. And it arranged an exhibition of quilts in conjunction with the world premier of *Gabriel's Daughter* at the Central City Opera House. The 2003 opera is the story of Aunt Clara Brown, a former slave who immigrated to Central City and helped other slaves come west.

"The majority of those quilts at Central City were made by African Americans, but they're not consequently African-American quilts," said Jessica Vaughan, introducing a subject Wa Shonaji members are passionate about.

"What's an African-American quilt?" asks Ida Schenck. "If it was made by an African American, it's an African-American quilt."

"I'm an African American, but I don't make African-American quilts," scoffs Julia Payne.

The women resist the idea that the boldly graphic but poorly constructed quilts made in some American black communities are indigenous to their culture. "Most of us don't do that. We don't want to," said Jessica. One Wa Shonaji member pointed to a magazine article referring to such work as "improvisational" African-American quilts. "Who called them that?" asked a woman. "Some white man," came a reply,

Iris Hawkins works on one of the comfort quilts that Wa Shonaji gives to those in need.

and everyone roared with laughter. The women admitted that some African Americans do make quilts that are shoddy and out-of-shape, but so do white quilters. And blacks, they point out, also make exquisite quilts, using contemporary designs and the latest cutting and sewing techniques. "We do have a culture. Some of us identify with it, some of us don't. Even we don't agree with each other," said Helen. Added Ida, "We're not all cut out of the same cloth." No, they're not.[i]

[i] Sandra Dallas, interviews, Denver, August 2, 2003.

Brenda Ames, Nannette Locke, and Glen Lyday stitch comfort quilts.

would infect me and want me to buy yarns," Patty laughed. She wanted to form an art quilt organization because "you need to have the camaraderie, the support, the constructive criticism," she explained. Front Range now has 200 members in Colorado and neighboring states and as far away as England, and it has made Colorado an important part of the art quilt movement. In addition to six meetings a year, Front Range sponsors workshops and holds at least one important show a year. Its 2003 Elements from the Front Range Contemporary Quilt Organization became a traveling exhibit.

"The cat's out of the bag. There's just no stopping this art quilt movement," said Patty Hawkins.[27] But then, that appears to be true of quilting in general. When they opened Quilts in the Attic in 1976, Marge Hedges and her partners thought the shop might be good for a few years, until women got bored with quilting and went on to something else. "We had no idea what would happen. Once they got turned on to quilting, you couldn't turn them off," Marge said.[28] Women and men discovered that quilting filled their lives in good times and bad, just as it had in generations past. "The best thing to do when the wind blows and the tumbleweeds fly is to go into the sewing room and bury yourself in your fabric stack and tackle another quilt," said Bonnie McFadden, a quilter in Sedgwick, on the Colorado–Nebraska border.[29] "There's no pulling back or dropping back," insisted Ricky Tims.[30] Quilting is "the love and the work I will leave behind." For today's quilters, he couldn't have said it better.

Colorado Quilting Council member Karen Brown examines a Boston Common Set with Vines in Fairplay, 2000, in a program that had documented more than 9,500 Colorado quilts by 2003.

Binding Off

Rocky Mountain Quilts

"People . . . brought their quilting habits with them."

Mary Ann Schmidt

Just a year after gold was discovered at the confluence of the South Platte River and the Cherry Creek, Susan and Stephen Adair, newlyweds from Missouri, arrived at the Cherry Creek Diggings, most likely in an oxen-drawn covered wagon piled high with their belongings. In 1859, the diggings, which only a short time before had been formalized under the name Denver, was a clutter of misshapen log and frame buildings on rutted dirt streets. There were more saloons than churches, more gambling "hells" than theaters. The fledgling city boasted a newspaper, the *Rocky Mountain News,* which is still being published, but little in the way of culture or refinement.

Golden History, 1992, made by some 30 quilters, Golden, Colo. Cottons, machine- and hand-appliquéd, machine- and hand-pieced, and hand-quilted, 62½″ × 82¾″. The quilt depicts Golden in its pioneer days.

Just why the Adairs sought their fortune in Denver and the gold camps in the mountains to the west is unknown. It's also unclear whether they came alone. Stephen had at least one child by a previous marriage, and later on, his father, a Tyrolean immigrant, lived with the couple.

What is known is that Susan brought with her blocks that she had made for a quilt. Some 135 years later, quilt historian Jeananne Wright discovered a quilt with a note attached to it: "The center blocks were made by Mrs. S.C. Adair and quilted with one of the first Howe sewing machines to come to Colorado Territory in 1859. The borders were added in 1917."

The note, which is not in Susan's hand since she was illiterate, identified the bold appliquéd design of yellow and red flowers and green leaves as "Jennie Linn." Today, quilters call the pattern Coxcomb or Princess Feather, but pattern names changed as quilters reworked them to fit familiar locations and events. So Coxcomb might once have been called Jennie Linn by someone besotted with the Swedish-born singer Jenny Lind. Or perhaps Susan had a friend Jennie Linn, who had loaned her the pattern. This is all speculation—like so much in quilt history is speculation.

Jeananne believes that Susan and the women in her family made the blocks for Susan's wedding quilt, possibly in preparation for the long journey to Denver. "Missouri, where she came from, has a history of incredible quilters during this time," Jeananne said. "The appliqué is meticulously done by hand. I believe she brought the blocks unfinished with her on the trail to the gold fields."

The couple eventually moved to Black Hawk, west of Denver, where Stephen became a toll gate keeper. Most men did not come west in those early days to guard roads, so Stephen probably tried his hand at prospecting, and perhaps while he hunted for gold, Susan completed her quilt. "The appliqué is double-stitched with a very old

Jeananne Wright with Susan Adair's Jennie Linn, the first documented quilt or quilt top in Colorado.

Colorado Wildflowers, 1974, made by Eugenia Mitchell, Golden, Colo. Cottons, machine-pieced, hand-embroidered, and hand-quilted, 84″ × 108″. The quilt hung in Colorado Senator Timothy Wirth's office in Washington, D.C.

and early machine and is exquisitely done. I think she did the interior of the quilt early on in Colorado, and then it was set aside as she took up a life in the gold mining camps and towns—and finished it in 1917, when she would have been in her later years," suggested Jeananne.

The machine quilting in the border was done by a later sewing machine. The fabrics in the original blocks are overdyed with vegetable dyes, first yellow, then blue, to create green, for instance, while the later, border fabrics are synthetically dyed. "Oh, how she must have disliked the green she had to use for the border," Jeananne said.[1]

Susan would have been typical of the women who came west. Unwilling to leave behind her precious quilt blocks with their memories of home in Missouri, Susan tucked them into the wagon for the trip across the prairie. She undoubtedly brought with her scraps of fabrics and designs that were popular at home. Susan was a skilled quilter, which was not unusual in those days, and she would have gotten pleasure from the artistry and skill she put into her work—but, like most quilters, she probably attached only a little importance to it. Women's work was always undervalued.

Still, two things about Susan stand out. At a time when art produced by women was usually anonymous, Susan's name has come down through history with her quilt. And Susan Adair's Jennie Linn is the first recorded quilt or quilt top to arrive in Colorado.

"No Unique Style"

Like Susan Adair, Colorado's quilters were typical of their time. They were not unique. Colorado did not produce a distinctive style of quilting. The state's first quilters brought their fabrics and their patterns with them, sharing their scraps and their designs with other pioneer women. "A lot of quilts came in covered wagons from other parts of the country," said Mary Ann Schmidt, head of the Colorado Quilting Council's Documentation Project. The project, begun in the mid-1980s, had documented some 9,500 quilts by 2004. Only a few are embellished with western elements, such as cattle brands, and most of those are of recent vintage.

"There is no unique style because people came here from other parts of the U.S. and brought their quilting habits with them. The early quilts are typical—Caesar's Crown, for instance—old blocks that came from the East," Mary Ann said. Besides, "those quilters didn't have time" to produce a unique style.[2]

Life was a struggle for pioneer women, who faced the demands of caring for themselves and their families under primitive conditions. They lived in log cabins and sod houses, most making do with the few belongings they had brought with them in covered wagons. Those who settled on the plains had the backbreaking work of carving farms out of the dry land, while gold-camp women washed clothes with buckets of water hauled up mountainsides from icy streams, and cooked over open fires. Pioneer women were called upon to administer to their community's sick and to provide a measure of culture, as well. Those first quilts made in the West were crude and utilitarian, fashioned with squares or brick-shape patches often cut from wool clothing. Who, indeed, had time for fancy stitching?

"Quilts are not a frontier kind of thing," said quilt historian Barbara Brackman, who has written extensively about quilts in Kansas and other western states. "People brought them in from the East, and when they used those up, they made new quilts." Although Kansas was settled in 1854, the state has no evidence of quilt making until 1875, she added.[3]

Another reason that Colorado boasts no indigenous quilting style is that the state was settled midway through America's quilt history. "Whole cloth was never made in Colorado. Medallion never came here. New England's four-poster chintz beauties were so much earlier," said Jeananne Wright.[4] And when Colorado women did begin making quilts, commercial patterns (and fabrics) were readily available. *Godey's Lady's Book* and *Peterson's Magazine* had published quilt designs for years. "The tradition of quilting was stronger than there being a regional style," said Alisa Zahller, Associate Curator for Decorative and Fine Arts at the Colorado Historical Society.[5] So Colorado quilters embraced national patterns and fads instead of developing their own.

Finally, Colorado did not produce a distinctive state design because its quilters were not a cohesive group. Colorado was a sparsely populated land of mountains and plains, with women living in pockets of settlement—a few cities and isolated mining towns and rural communities. The Keota Quilters of Northeast Colorado, women who lived on farms near the town of Keota, for instance, lived too far from each other to get together often for quilting bees.[6] And the patterns the women in that area chose were traditional ones. The quilters were as likely to have brought patterns with them from the East or copied them out of magazines as to have borrowed designs from each other.

A Lifetime of Quilts—Eugenia Mitchell

Ninety-seven years after Susan Adair and her Jennie Linn quilt squares reached Denver by covered wagon, Eugenia Mitchell arrived in the city in a Cadillac automobile. Like Susan's prairie schooner, Eugenia's Cadillac most likely held a scrap bag of quilt pieces, probably in the back seat, where it was in easy reach.

Despite the passage of nearly a century, Eugenia had much in common with Susan—and with the other quilters who came west in the intervening years. She was frugal, using fabric she had on hand and spending little money on new supplies. She did not embrace any one style but selected designs that utilized the fabric she had on hand. She picked patterns that appealed to her, many of them fashionable, even faddish. She was proud of her work, although others, men mostly, still didn't consider quilting much more than making bedcovers. And Eugenia quilted whenever she could, snatching precious moments from her household duties. Like her predecessors, in fact, Eugenia undoubtedly pieced her quilts as she crossed the prairie beside her husband, although the Cadillac covered in a day the miles that took pioneers weeks to traverse behind plodding oxen.

Eugenia and her husband Elmer passed through Denver and went to Golden, where her brother Ruben Hartmeister worked for the Adolph Coors Company, the brewery. Elmer found work painting a church, and the couple used the $125 he made from the work as a down payment on a house at 1414 Washington Avenue in Golden. Elmer got a full-time job painting tract houses, while Eugenia set up housekeeping and scoured Golden for cheap real estate to purchase. In the moments she could find after working as a domestic and cooking for boarders, Eugenia took out her fabric scraps and her patterns and, like Susan Adair, she quilted her way into Colorado history.

Eugenia Hartmeister had begun quilting at the age of ten. "I learned to quilt at my mother's knee,

Halley's Comet Signature, 1977, made by Eugenia Mitchell, Golden, Colo. Cottons, machine-pieced and hand-quilted, 82¼″ × 93″. The quilt contains 506 signatures.

The Hartmeister children, with Eugenia, age 15, second from right.

for Mother always quilted. Since I was such a tomboy, Mother thought quilting would be a nice, lady-like thing for me to do. By the time I got married, I had made four quilts for my future home. I've lost count of how many I've made in the years since," she recalled. "My creativity comes from Mother, which came from her father. He invented a machine to shell filbert nuts."[7]

Eugenia's parents were Lutheran missionaries in Brazil, where she was born October 13, 1903, the oldest surviving of twelve children; six lived. The family returned to the United States when Eugenia was two, and she was raised in Illinois, dropping out of school in the ninth grade to work as a mother's helper. In 1924, at age 20, Eugenia married Ray Mitchell—both of her husbands were Mitchells, although they were not related—and the couple went to South Dakota so that Ray could work on the Lincoln Highway. They lived in a home-made trailer attached to a hayrack. When Ray was laid off, the two moved to Storm Lake, Iowa.

Marriage was not easy for Eugenia, who ran a farm while Ray worked in a lumber yard. "Ray was a home person, but he thought home was for eating and sleeping, and the wife raising the family. Every evening, he played pool for an hour-and-a-half, read the paper, and went to bed. There was no moral support for me," Eugenia said. In addition to raising four children and keeping house, Eugenia milked cows, killed chickens, tended a garden, and each year, put up as many as 1,000 jars of vegetables, meat, sauerkraut, and tomato juice, and gallons of molasses and honey. She cut up old clothes for quilts, then tore the parts too worn for quilts into strips for rugs. She wove the rugs on a hand-pegged loom that she had found in a chicken house and purchased for $10. Eugenia also took outside jobs doing laundry and housework.

With all the hard work and a lack of support at home, Eugenia, at age 32, developed crippling arthritis and was on the verge of a nervous breakdown. A psychiatrist told her to "eliminate the problem"—and that was Ray, she said. So Eugenia separated from her husband, eventually divorcing him. And her health returned.

Ray still supported the family. He called every Sunday and handed Eugenia $20. "But if there were five Sundays in a month, he didn't show up and didn't pay another $20," she said. Ray died not long after the divorce, and at his funeral, Eugenia discovered that her husband had been married before he met her and had had two children by his first wife. "I felt we would have been married till the day he died but for his hidden secrets, like the hidden stars in the Hidden Star quilt," she said.

While she raised her children and took in boarders, Eugenia found a job with the Bemis Brothers Bag Company, sewing duffle bags. Later, she worked at home, slaughtering chickens. She could kill, dress, and draw 250 chickens in eight hours. In 1949, Eugenia married one of her boarders, Elmer Mitchell. Three years later, the couple moved to Golden. The marriage was a happy one, Eugenia claimed, although Elmer was an alcoholic and had trouble holding a job because of his drinking. Several years after the couple moved to Golden, Elmer was bitten by a snake and died from the effects of the venom.

American Flag, c. 1979, made by Eugenia Mitchell, Golden, Colo. Cottons, machine-pieced and hand-quilted, 81¼″ × 83¼″. Eugenia's son rescued red-white-and-blue bunting from a Kirkwood, Missouri, dump after a July 4, 1943 celebration. Eugenia combined it with discarded flags collected in 1979 from the Golden cemetery.

Alone again, Eugenia, who had no further use for husbands, remained in Golden, cleaning houses, caring for the sick, and quilting—always quilting. "She became obsessive about quilts," said her daughter Mary Ellen Gray. "Maybe that's because they didn't give her any trouble."[8]

Among Eugenia's first quilts, one of the four she made before she married Ray Mitchell, was an all-wool quilt, pieced from gray, brown, and pink patches cut from worn-out dresses. The backing and ties were wool, and so was the batting. Eugenia, then eighteen, was working in a dry goods store when she made the quilt, and she asked a salesman to recommend the best quality batting for her quilt. He told her to use lamb's wool, which sold for $35 a batt (cotton batting went for $1.50 then). "I was making $35 a month, so I just told the boss man to order me a batch of lamb's wool and take it out of my pay," said Eugenia, who used the quilt for more than fifty years, until 1981.

Like most Colorado pioneer women, Eugenia generally did not produce show quilts. She made serviceable bedcovers, using scraps left over from dressmaking or cut from worn-out clothing. That is not to say that Eugenia's quilts were dull. She used bright colors and fabrics and eye-catching designs. After Elmer died, she pieced a Drunkard's Path. "I didn't choose that with my husband in mind—or maybe I did," she said.

Eugenia's quilting skills were unexceptional, but her imagination set her apart as a quilter. Some quilts, Eugenia said, "I made from patterns, some I've bought and repaired, some were given to me to finish, and others are made from my own original designs." Those designs usually were inspired by what she had on hand. She made a quilt of colorful women's handkerchiefs, setting them on point, for instance. Another quilt was pieced from discarded flags and bunting salvaged from patriotic celebrations. Eugenia cut and pieced the bunting and used it as a backdrop for a large American flag, and

Eugenia's Doilies, 1975, made by Eugenia Mitchell, Golden, Colo. Cotton blends, machine-pieced, hand-appliquéd, and hand-quilted, 73½" × 89". The quilt includes 25 yards of tatting that Eugenia found in a Goodwill store and doilies she purchased for five to 25 cents.

Duck's Foot in the Mud (Bear Paw variation), 1976, assembled by Eugenia Mitchell, Golden, Colo., quilted by Teresa and Mary Rose Schultz, Calhoun, Ky. Cottons and cotton blends, machine- and hand-pieced and hand-quilted, 79½″ × 88½″. Eugenia purchased the blocks at a yard sale in Golden in 1970.

when the bunting proved to be scant, she inserted a piece of red-and-white striped fabric—just as quilters before her had made do when they ran out of material. "She loved to go to second-hand stores and find old, beat-up quilts and refurbish them. And she made quilts out of neckties and doilies she found there," recalled her longtime friend Teri DuBois.[9] "Eugenia could take a tablecloth and put strips around it and make it into a really wonderful quilt," said Mary Ann Schmidt.[10]

She quilted tops made by others, charging $125 for a full-size quilt, which generally took five days of hand-stitching to complete. An average quilt, she said, had 60,000 stitches. Eugenia stitched those quilts holding her needle between her thumb and first finger of her left hand, although she wrote with her right hand. She made her own lye soap for washing quilts. (She insisted that the Rocky Mountain Quilt Museum gift shop stock the soap, but volunteers quietly warned quilters the stuff was harsh.)

In the 1970s, as America's quilt revival got underway, Eugenia, who had begun teaching quilting, was recognized for her quilts. Her work was exhibited in a 1973 show at the Denver Art Museum. She often packed her quilts into four suitcases and four trunks and loaded them into her car, then drove across the country to participate in shows and seminars, becoming well known as a folk artist. "I don't know what I am," she countered, when someone tried to categorize her. "I just like working with quilts." She opened her own quilt store in Golden, once selling a Lone Star quilt for $450. Her

Eugenia started the Rocky Mountain Quilt Museum with a donation of 100 quilts.

Hiwan Homestead, 1979, made by Eugenia Mitchell, Golden, Colo. Cottons and cotton blends, machine- and hand-pieced and hand-quilted, 79" × 94" inches. Eugenia sat on a stone bench in front of the old homestead and drew the house. The quilt hung in the Hiwan Homestead Museum, Evergreen, Colo.

Wildflowers, 1981, made by Eugenia Mitchell, Golden, Colo. Cottons, machine- and hand-appliquéd, hand-embroidered, and hand-quilted, 74" × 92". The flowers were copied from Denver Post designs for textile painting.

The Quilt That Walked to Golden

work was displayed in shop windows in Golden, where, dressed in patchwork skirts and vests and even shoes, her hair hanging down her back in two gray braids, Eugenia was a familiar figure. "She was pretty spicy," said Marie Overdier, who began quilting with Eugenia in 1972. "She was a real go-getter, I'll tell you that."[11]

Over the years, Eugenia acquired what she considered a museum-quality collection of quilts. "She was ahead of her time. She realized that the historical significance of what she saw represented a lot of Colorado history, and she wanted to pass it on," said Mary Ann Schmidt.[12] In 1981, Eugenia invited a group of women to meet in Golden to organize the Rocky Mountain Quilt Museum. It was begun with 100 of Eugenia's quilts. When the museum opened its doors in 1990, Eugenia worked as a volunteer, escorting people through the displays of quilts—usually ones that Eugenia had collected or made herself.

And she continued to quilt. "I'm always working on a quilt, either finishing one someone else started and didn't finish, or designing and making new ones, or repairing quilts that I buy from the Salvation Army and Goodwill" for as little as ten cents, she said. At night, she slept with an unfinished quilt spread over her so that when she awoke during the night, she could stitch until she fell asleep again. "I'll probably be threading a needle or sewing on a quilt when I breathe my last," she said.

That was not to be. In 1999, Eugenia was institutionalized with Alzheimer's Disease, and her quilting ceased. Even then, however, she never completely forgot about the work that had come to dominate her life. On her better days, Eugenia would tell a worker at the home that she was making her a quilt. One day, the woman prodded Eugenia, asking, "Didn't you say you were making me a quilt for Christmas?" Eugenia, who was 100 in 2003 when this book went to press, brightened, and a part of her old self came back. "Yes," she replied. "But I didn't say which year."[13]

Four Traditional Quilt Patterns

Pioneer quiltmakers brought their patterns with them on the Overland Trail, precious cardboard or paper shapes tucked into scrap bags and work baskets. Over the years, Colorado quilters did not create their own designs but embraced and embellished those borrowed from friends or copied from popular women's magazines. The four patterns included here, adapted by Cindy Harp from quilts in the Rocky Mountain Quilt Museum, are among the best-loved quilt designs not only in Colorado but in America. Note that the patterns are brief and assume a basic knowledge of piecing and appliqué techniques. For extra help, choose from among the many excellent books on quilting available at your local fabric shop, book store, or library.

This Sampler Quilt by Cindy Harp incorporates four traditional quilt blocks. A pattern for each follows.

Courthouse Steps quilt top, c. 1890, maker unknown. Cottons and wools, foundation-pieced by machine, 59″ × 88½″.

Courthouse Steps

Since most early Colorado dwellings were made of pine logs chinked with mud, no quilt pattern was more appropriate for westering Americans than Log Cabin, of which Courthouse Steps is a popular variation. The center square traditionally is red to represent the hearth, the heart of the home. And the blocks themselves are arranged in patterns that represent pioneer life—Barn Raising, Sunshine and Shadow, Windmill Blades, and Streak O' Lightning.

The quilt shown here has 150 blocks, set 10 × 15. With a block size of 6⅛", the finished quilt, adapted from the antique quilt shown opposite, measures 61" × 76". Read all directions carefully before you begin. Seam allowances of ¼" are included in all measurements.

Yardage

Assorted lights: 4½ to 5 yds   Assorted darks: 4½ to 5 yds

Cutting

For each block, cut:

#1 3 squares   1⅜" × 1⅜"   #4 2 rectangles 1⅜" × 4⅞"
#2 2 rectangles 1⅜" × 3⅛"   #5 2 rectangles 1⅜" × 4⅞"
#3 2 rectangles 1⅜" × 3⅛"   #6 2 rectangles 1⅜" × 6⅝"

Sewing

1. Piece each block according to diagram, working from center of block outwards. For multiple blocks or strip piecing, cut variety of 1⅜" strips. Piece three #1 squares together, then add strips in order shown, trimming as each strip is attached.

2. Sew blocks together into rows.

3. Sew rows together.

4. Quilt and bind as desired.

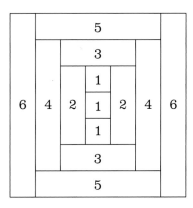

Schoolhouse, 1950, maker unknown, Pennsylvania (?). Cottons, machine-pieced and hand-quilted, 45¾″ × 74″.

Schoolhouse

Americans went west for a better life, and part of that better life was education. It was natural, then, that the schoolhouse with its board siding and bell tower not only was the first public building erected in many communities, but the finest. Settlers brought their architectural ideas with them, so a school in a Colorado prairie town might look just like one in Maine. And a Schoolhouse quilt pieced in the West looked remarkably like one made in the East.

The quilt shown here has 15 blocks, set 3 × 5. With a block size of 8½″ and a sashing/border width of 2½″, the finished quilt, adapted from the antique quilt shown opposite, measures 40½″ × 62½″. Read all directions carefully before you begin. Seam allowances of ¼″ are included in all measurements. Templates (see page 152) are full size and include seam allowance.

Yardage

Background: 1½ yds

Chimney: ½ yd

Roof: 1 yd

House: 2¼ yds

Window: 1 yd

Sashing and border: 2½ yds

Cornerstones and star points: 1 yd

Cutting

For each block, cut:

Background

#1 1 rectangle   2⅜″ × 3¼″

#2 1 rectangle   2⅛″ × 1⅝″

#3 2 Templates A (reverse for 1)

Chimne and Background

#4 3 rectangles 2⅛″ × 1⅞″

Roof

#5 1 Template B

#6 1 Template C

House and Windows

#7 2 rectangles   1¾″ × 6¼″

#8 2 rectangles   1¾″ × 3¼″

#9 3 rectangles   2⅛″ × 1¼″

#10 3 rectangles   2⅛″ × 1⅜″

Door

#11 1 rectangle   2⅛″ × 1½″

Women made templates from cereal boxes or other cardboard containers.

The Quilt That Walked to Golden

Sashing for 15 block quilt

38 strips	$3'' \times 9''$
76 squares	$1\frac{3}{4}'' \times 1\frac{3}{4}''$, cut diagonally into half-square triangles
24 cornerstone squares	$3'' \times 3''$

Borders

| Top and bottom | 2 strips | $3'' \times 41''$ |
| Sides | 2 strips | $3'' \times 58''$ |

Sewing

1. Piece each block according to diagram.
2. Sew two half-square triangles as shown to each end of sashing strips, trimming away excess strip fabric.
3. Piece cornerstone squares to sashing strips, using photograph as guide.
4. Sew blocks/sashing together into rows
5. Sew rows together.
6. Quilt and bind as desired.

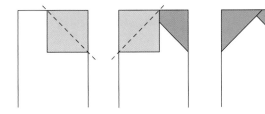

Hands All Around, 2003, block maker unknown, quilted by Last Chance Quilters, Last Chance, Colo. Cottons, hand- and machine-pieced, and hand-quilted, 50″ × 68½″. The antique blocks were purchased on the Internet, then assembled and quilted.

The Quilt That Walked to Golden

Hands All Around

Living in remote mining camps or on isolated farms and ranches, Colorado women relished the opportunity to come together to quilt. Pioneer accounts are filled with the joy of quilting bees—the colorful quilts, gossip, dinner. Later women helped each other through hard times as they met over their needles. Hands All Around, the symbol of the Rocky Mountain Quilt Museum, represents Colorado's community of quilters.

This quilt, inspired by the antique quilt shown opposite, measures 48″ × 65″. With a block size of 14″, the finished quilt has 12 blocks, set 3 × 4, with 3″ sashing strips. Read all directions carefully before you begin. Seam allowances of ¼″ are included on all templates (see pages 153–154).

Yardage

Light: 3½ yds   Dark: 2¼ yds

Cutting

For each block, cut from background fabric:

Template A   Cut 1   Template C   Cut 8   Template E   Cut 8

For each block, cut from contrast fabric:

Template B   Cut 4   Template D   Cut 16

Sashing

8 strips   3½″ × 14½″   3 strips   3½″ × 48½″

Sewing

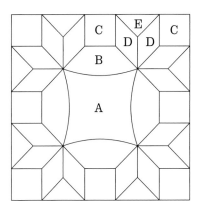

1. Sew D to DR, then set in E to complete unit. Make 8.
2. Join two units from Step 1 along diagonal, as shown in the layout diagram. Set in square C to complete corner unit. Make 4.
3. Sew remaining C squares to B pieces. Make four. Sew each BC piece into a curved side of piece A.
4. Sew corner units from Step 2 to large ABC unit.
5. Set sashing strips between blocks, then between rows.
6. Quilt and bind as desired.

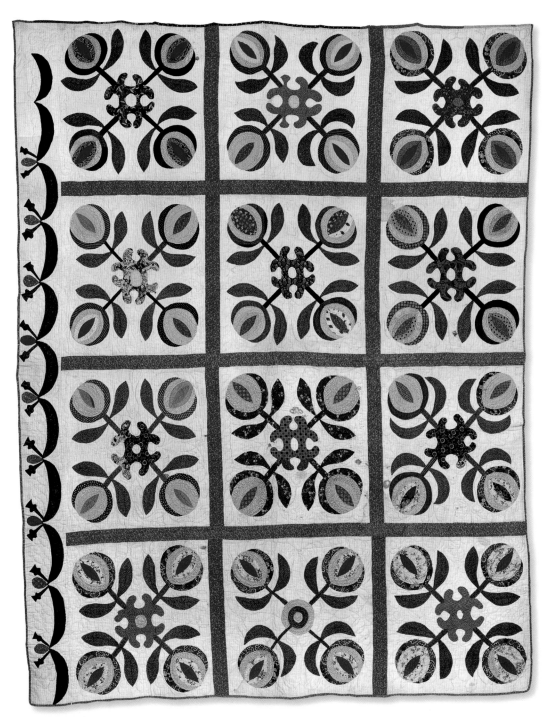

Pomegranate or Love Apple, 1860–1865, made by Mrs. Benjamin Franklin Buckner, Madison County, Va. Cottons, hand-appliquéd and hand-quilted, 79¼" × 99". The swag is on only one side, probably because the bed was shoved against a wall. An accomplished whistler, Benjamin, who rode with Jeb Stuart during the Civil War, performed for Confederate troops.

The Quilt That Walked to Golden

Pomegranate

The first quilts made in the West were serviceable ones, hastily assembled by busy women with no time for fancy sewing. But the women brought with them exquisite quilts made in such designs as Pomegranate, or Love Apple, to remind them of home and to serve as inspiration for future needlework.

The pattern that follows, inspired by the antique quilt shown opposite, measures 70½″ × 94″, without borders. With a block size of 23½″, there are 12 blocks, set 3 × 4. Read all directions carefully before you begin. Seam allowances are not included in the templates (see pages 155–156). Add ¼″ or ⅛″ seam allowance to each piece before cutting.

Yardage

Background	8 yds	Pomegranate piece E	¼ yd
Center	1½ yds	Pomegranate piece F	½ yd
Stems and		Pomegranate piece G	1 yd
leaves	1¼ yds	Pomegranate piece H	2 yds

Cutting

For each block, cut:

Background square	Cut 1 24″ × 24″	Template D	Cut 8 (reverse for 4)
Template A	Cut 1 on fold	Template E	Cut 4
Template B	Cut 1	Template F	Cut 4
Template C	Cut 4	Template G	Cut 4
		Template H	Cut 4

Sewing

1. Press background square on diagonal for ease of design placement. Lightly mark around templates to transfer design to fabric.
2. Appliqué circle A in place. Pin large piece B and stem C in position. Appliqué leaves D, then stem C. Appliqué B. Next, appliqué pomegranate pieces E, F, G, and H in that order.
3. If desired, add sashing and borders.
4. Quilt and bind as desired.

Schoolhouse Templates

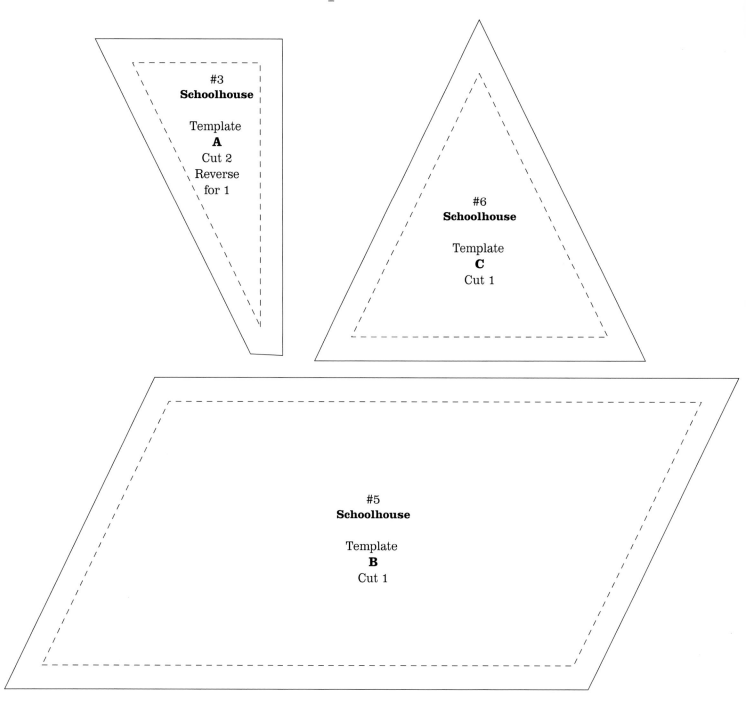

#3
Schoolhouse

Template
A
Cut 2
Reverse
for 1

#6
Schoolhouse

Template
C
Cut 1

#5
Schoolhouse

Template
B
Cut 1

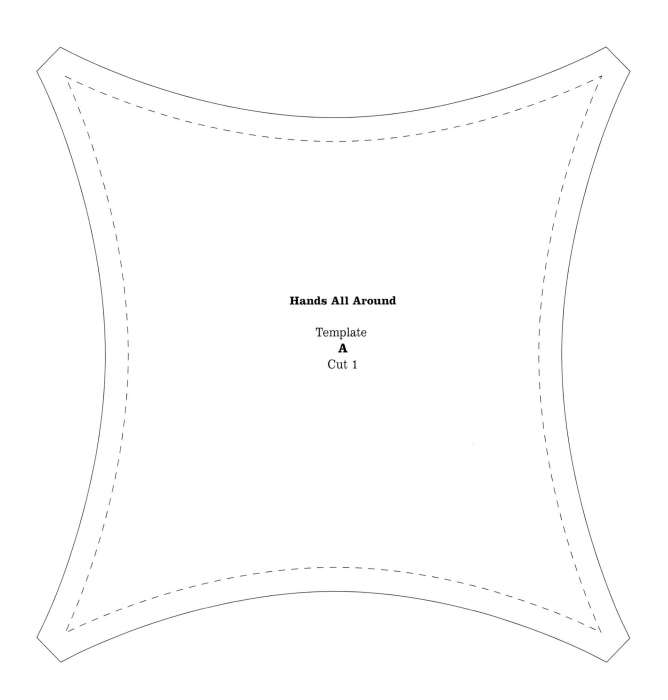

Hands All Around

Template
A
Cut 1

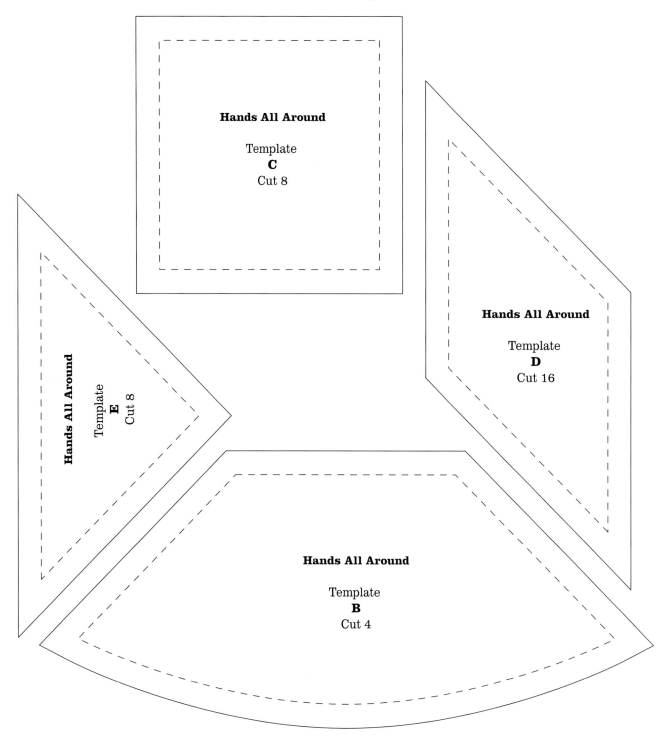

Hands All Around

Template
C
Cut 8

Hands All Around

Template
D
Cut 16

Hands All Around

Template
E
Cut 8

Hands All Around

Template
B
Cut 4

Pomegranate Templates

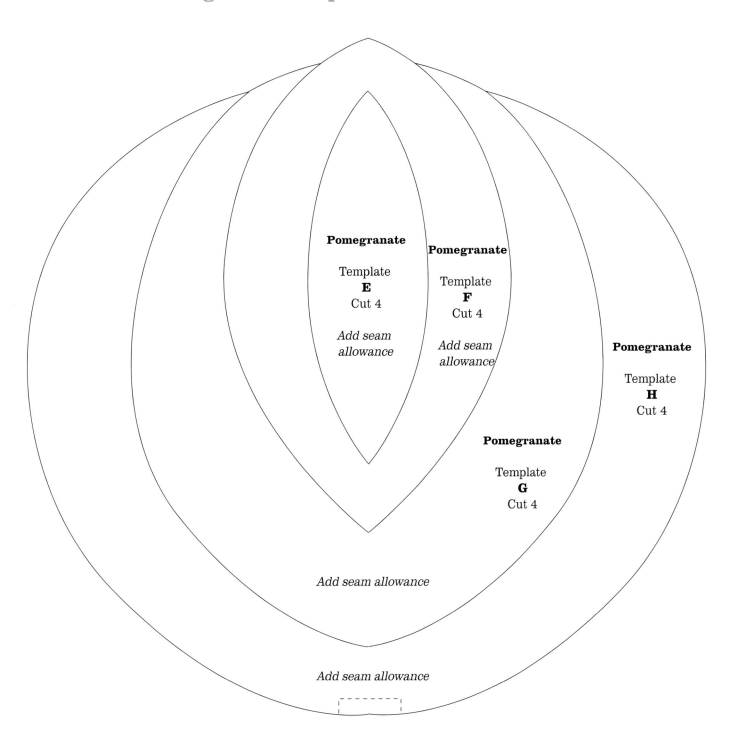

Pomegranate

Template
E
Cut 4

*Add seam
allowance*

Pomegranate

Template
F
Cut 4

*Add seam
allowance*

Pomegranate

Template
H
Cut 4

Pomegranate

Template
G
Cut 4

Add seam allowance

Add seam allowance

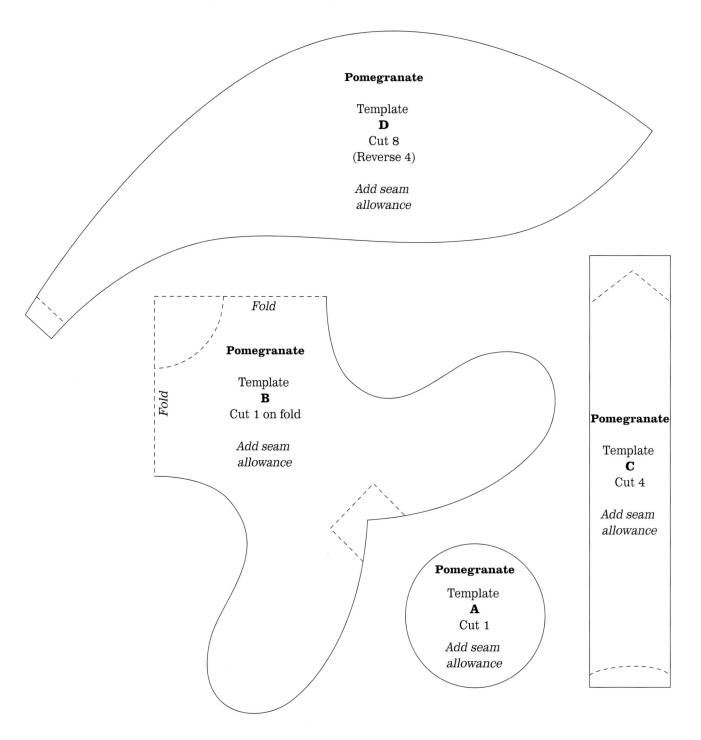

Pomegranate

Template
D
Cut 8
(Reverse 4)

*Add seam
allowance*

Fold

Fold

Pomegranate

Template
B
Cut 1 on fold

*Add seam
allowance*

Pomegranate

Template
C
Cut 4

*Add seam
allowance*

Pomegranate

Template
A
Cut 1

*Add seam
allowance*

Notes

The Quilt That Walked to Golden

1. Mary Fanning, *For the Golden Times*, (Denver: John Waddell Press, 1977,) 6–11.

2. Colorado Quilting Council Historical Documentation Interview Sheet, RMQ-1079, 4 Mar. 1991.

Westering

1. Sandra Dallas, *Gold and Gothic*, (Denver: Lick Skillet Press, 1967,) 1–4, 11.

2. Ibid., 1.

3. [?] Pratt and [?] Hunt, *Guide to the Gold Mines of Kansas*, (Chicago: self-published, 1859,) 21.

4. L. Maria Child, *The Girl's Own Book*, (New York: Clark Austin & Co., 1834,) 203, 225.

5. L. Maria Child, *The American Frugal Housewife*, (New York: Samuel S. & William Wood, 1838,) 1, 4.

6. Sarah Jane Hale, ed., *Good Little Girls' Book*, (New York: McLoughlin Bros., n.d.,) 15, 22.

7. Susan G. Butruille, *Women's Voices from the Western Frontier*, (Boise: Tamarack Books Inc., 1995,) 187.

8. A.W. Chase, *Dr. Chase's Recipes; or, Information for Everybody: An Invaluable Collection of about Eight Hundred Practical Recipes*, (Ann Arbor: self-published, 1865,) 347–8.

9. Katherine Harris, *Long Vistas: Women and Families on Colorado Homesteads*, (Niwot: University Press of Colorado, 1993,) 85.

10. Kenneth L. Holmes and David C. Duniway, eds., *Covered Wagon Women: Diaries & Letters from the Western Trails 1840–1890*, 11 vols. (Glendale: Arthur H. Clark Co., 1983–1993,) 5:27, 29–30.

11. Anonymous, *Hand Book to the Gold Fields of Nebraska and Kansas. Being a Complete Guide to the Gold Regions of the South Platte & Cherry Creek*, (Chicago: D.B. Cooke & Co., 1859,) 22, 28.

12. James Redpath and Richard J. Hinton, *Hand-Book to Kansas Territory and the Rocky Mountains' Gold Region*, (New York: J.H. Colton, 1859,) 31, 144.

13. [?] Reed, *Reed's Guide to the Kansas Gold Region*, (New York: J.H. Colton, 1859,) 8.

14. Linda Peavy and Ursula Smith, *The Gold Rush Widows of Little Falls*, (St. Paul: Minnesota Historical Society Press, 1990,) 161.

15. Julia Archibald Holmes, *A Bloomer Girl on Pike's Peak 1858*, Agnes Wright Spring, ed., (Denver: Western History Dept., Denver Public Library, 1949,) 30–31.

16. Mary Hayden, *Pioneer Days*, (Fairfield, Wash.: Ye Galleon Press, 1979,) 9–10.

17. Alice Polk Hill, *Tales of the Colorado Pioneers*, (Glorieta, New Mexico: The Rio Grande Press Inc., 1976,) 222.

18. Caroline Bancroft, *Augusta Tabor: Her Side of the Scandal*, (Boulder: Johnson Publishing Co., 1955) and *Silver Queen: The Fabulous Story of Baby Doe Tabor*, (Boulder: Johnson Publishing Co., 1950.)

19. *Covered Wagon Women: Diaries & Letters from the Western Trails 1840–1890*, 1:213-4.

20. Ibid., 7:15, 24.

21. Ibid., 1:213, 216–7.

22. Orpha Baldwin McNitt and Alice McNitt Montgomery, *Letters from a Frontier Bride and Prairie Christmas and Other Stories*, (No city, no publisher, 1993,) 29.

23. Lillian Schlissel, *Women's Diaries of the Westward Journey*, (New York: Schocken Books, 1982,) 203.

24. *Covered Wagon Women: Diaries & Letters from the Western Trails 1840–1890*, 6:52.

25. Ibid., 6:269.

26. Sandra L. Myres, ed., *Ho For California!: Women's Overland Diaries from the Huntington Library*, (San Marino: Huntington Library, 1980,) 100.

27. *Covered Wagon Women: Diaries & Letters from the Western Trails 1840–1890*, 1:68–9.

28. Ibid., 7:58.

29. Lucy Rutledge Cooke, *Crossing the Plains in 1852: Narrative of a Trip From Iowa to "The Land of Gold," As Told in Letters Written During the Journey*, (Fairfield, Washington: Ye Galleon Press, n.d.,) 73.

30. Bert Webber, ed., *The Oregon & California Trail Dairy of Jane Gould in 1862*, (Medford: Webb Research Group, 1987,) 61–3.

31. Barbara Brackman, "Quilts on the Kansas Frontier," *Kansas History*, Vol. 13, No. 1, (Topeka: Kansas State Historical Society, Spring, 1990,) 21.

32. *Covered Wagon Women: Diaries & Letters from the Western Trails 1840–1890*, 8:153.

33. Ibid., 9:70.

34. Dale Morgan, Ed., *Overland in 1846: Diaries and Letters of the California-Oregon Trail*, Vol. II, (Georgetown, California: Talisman Press, 1963,) 474–5.

35. *Covered Wagon Women: Diaries & Letters from the Western Trails 1840–1890*, 3:142–3.

36. Ibid., 2:94.

37. Ibid., 7:72.

38. Jeanne Hamilton Watson, ed., *To the Land of Gold and Wickedness: The 1848–59 Diary of Lorena L. Hays*, (St. Louis: Patrice Press, 1988,) 150.

[39] *Covered Wagon Women: Diaries & Letters from the Western Trails 1840–1890*, 7:270.

[40] Eugene Smith, *Pioneer Epic*, (Boulder: Johnson Publishing Co., 1951,) 26–7.

[41] James L. Thane Jr., Ed., *A Governor's Wife on the Mining Frontier: The Letters of Mary Edgerton from Montana, 1863–1865*, (Salt Lake City: University of Utah Library, 1976,) 76.

[42] *Covered Wagon Women: Diaries & Letters from the Western Trails 1840–1890*, 1:58.

[43] Darlis A. Miller, *Mary Hallock Foote: Author-Illustrator of the American West*, (Norman: University of Oklahoma Press, 2002,) 38–9.

Settling In

[1] Mollie Dorsey Sanford, *Mollie: The Journal of Mollie Dorsey Sanford in Nebraska and Colorado Territories 1857–1866*, (Lincoln: University of Nebraska Press, 1959,) 68.

[2] Ibid., 135.

[3] Mollie Dorsey Sanford, "The Old Ranch Near Littleton, Colorado: Diary of Mollie Dorsey Sanford, May 2, 1895–March 19, 1900," unpublished manuscript, (Littleton: Littleton Historical Museum,) March 25, April 3, 6–7, 1897.

[4] Mollie Dorsey Sanford, *The Journal of Mollie Dorsey Sanford in Nebraska and Colorado Territories, 1857–1866*, 195.

[5] Hazel Denney, *Veteran, District 13: Homesteading in Goshen Hole*, (Philadelphia: Dorrance & Co., 1976,) 180.

[6] Barbara Brackman, "Quilts on the Kansas Frontier," *Kansas History*, Vol. 13., No. 1, (Topeka: Kansas State Historical Society, Spring, 1990,) 22.

[7] Georgia Schad, *Mary E. Hatfield LaFollette: My Pioneer Mother*, (Weiser: Commercial Printers & Publishers, 1954,) 5, 10, 14, 25, 32, 44.

[8] Jessie Babcock, unpublished journal, (Littleton: Littleton Historical Museum,) n.p.

[9] Mrs. Daniel Witter, "Pioneer Life," *The Colorado Magazine*, (Denver: The State Historical and Natural History Society of Colorado, Vol. IV, No. 5, December, 1927,) 169–170.

[10] Susan G. Butruille, *Women's Voices from the Western Frontier*, (Boise: Tamarack Books Inc., 1995,) 181.

[11] Mary Bywater Cross, *Treasures in the Trunk: Quilts of the Oregon Trail*, (Nashville: Rutledge Hill Press, 1993,) 84–85.

[12] Nellie Jean Nichols, unpublished journal, MSS1209, (Denver: Colorado Historical Society,) n.p.

[13] Anonymous, 1883, unpublished journal, Sandra Dallas collection.

[14] Orpha Baldwin McNitt and Alice McNitt Montgomery, *Letters from a Frontier Bride and Prairie Christmas and Other Stories*, n.p., 27.

[15] Nellie Jean Nichols, unpublished journal , n.p.

[16] Thomas Hornsby Ferril, "Magenta," *Westering*, (New Haven: Yale University Press, 1934,) 34–35.

[17] John Ise, *Sod and Stubble: The Story of a Kansas Homestead*, (Lincoln: University of Nebraska Press, 1936,) 1, 27, 297, 311.

[18] Anonymous, *Steadfast in Faith: A Book of Memories 1874–1999*, (Georgetown: First United Presbyterian Church, 1999,) 15.

[19] Nell Brown Propst, *Those Strenuous Dames of the Colorado Prairie*, (Boulder: Pruett Publishing Co., 1982,) 168.

[20] Emily French, *Emily: The Diary of a Hard-Worked Woman*, Janet Lecompte, ed., (Lincoln: University of Nebraska Press, 1987,) 2, 5, 10, 19, 24, 44, 50, 72, 74, 91, 111, 115, 119, 140.

[21] Ibid., 59.

[22] Ruth Brandon, *A Capitalist Romance: Singer and the Sewing Machine*, (Philadelphia: J.B. Lippincott Co., 1977,) 55, 58, 101.

[23] William Rush Dunton, Jr., *Old Quilts*, (Catonsville: self-published, 1946,) 56.

[24] Byrd Gibbens, ed., *This Is a Strange Country: Letters of a Westering Family, 1880–1906*, (Albuquerque: University of New Mexico Press, 1988,) 130.

[25] Agnes Just Reid, *Letters of Long Ago*, (Salt Lake City: Tanner Trust Fund, University of Utah Library, 1973,) 20, 24.

[26] Joanna L. Stratton, *Pioneer Women: Voices from the Kansas Frontier*, (New York: Simon and Schuster, 1981,) 213–214, 288.

[27] Sandra Dallas interview with Pat Hubbard, Denver, March 7, 2002.

[28] John Ise, *Sod and Stubble: The Story of a Kansas Homestead*, 60, 81–82, 101, 200.

[29] Evalyn Walsh McLean, *Father Struck It Rich*, (Boston: Little, Brown and Co., 1936,) 11, 136.

[30] Anonymous, "1st Sewing Machine Salesman," *Colorado Prospector*, Vol. 13, No. 6, June, 1982, (Englewood: Colorado Prospector Inc.,) 5.

[31] Sandra Dallas, interview with Alberta Iliff Shattuck, Englewood, Jan. 21, 2002.

[32] Ruth Brandon, *A Capitalist Romance: Singer and the Sewing Machine*, 128.

[33] Anonymous: *Rocky Mountain News*, June 26, 1869, 2.

[34] Sandra Dallas, interview with Alberta Iliff Shattuck, Englewood, Jan. 21, 2002.

[35] Sandra Dallas, interview with Rudy Giecek, Butte, June 26, 2003.

[36] Sandra Dallas, interview with Everett Parker, Denver, circa 1989.

[37] William W. Sanger, *The History of Prostitution: Its Extent, Causes and Effects Throughout the World*, (New York: Eugenics Publishing Co., 1939,) 552, 560.

[38] Maggie Jennings sewing book, n.p., Sandra Dallas collection.

[39] Joanna L. Stratton, *Pioneer Women: Voices from the Kansas Frontier*, 69.

[40] Sandra Dallas, interview with Margaret Geick, Denver, May 14, 2002.

[41] Anonymous, "Tumbling Blocks Autograph Quilt: Emma Schoefield Wright, c. 1880," H.6200.1268, Colorado Historical Society documentation.

[42] William Rush Dunton Jr., *Old Quilts*, 9.

[43] Ruth E. Finley, *Old Patchwork Quilts and the Women Who Made Them*, (no city: Charles T. Branford Co., 1929,) 32.

[44] Anonymous, "Colorado's Quilts and Quilters," *Colorado Prospector*, Vol. 13, No. 6, June 1982, 1.

[45] Anonymous, "Denver's Quilter," *Colorado Prospector*, Vol. 13, No. 6, June 1982, 2. Anonymous, "Crazy Quilt Florence Bell, 1890–93," H.2771.1. Colorado Historical Society documentation.

[46] John L. Bell letter, Jan. 25, 1904, Colorado Historical Society.

[47] Anonymous, "The Special Tabor Touch," *Colorado Prospector*, Vol. 13, No. 6, June 1982, 6.

[48] Hazel Green, 1885–86, unpublished journal. Sandra Dallas collection.

Hands All Around

[1] Anne Ellis, *The Life of an Ordinary Woman*, (Boston: Houghton Mifflin Co., 1929,) 56–57, 82.

[2] Anne Ellis, *Plain Anne Ellis: More About the Life of an Ordinary Woman*, (Lincoln: University of Nebraska Press, 1931,) 11–13, 15.

[3] Anne Ellis, *The Life of an Ordinary Woman*, 186.

4 Anne Ellis, *Plain Anne Ellis: More About the Life of an Ordinary Woman*, 103.

5 Belle Turnbull, "Window on the Street," *The Tenmile Range*, (Iowa City: Prairie Press, 1957,) 34.

6 Excerpt from "Goldboat" by Belle Turnbull. Copyright 1940 by Belle Turnbull. Copyright © renewed 1968 by Belle Turnbull. Reprinted by permission of Houghton Mifflin Co. All rights reserved.

7 O. Ray Dodson, ed., *The Promised—Land Homestead Memories*, (Pueblo: Prairie Heritage Press, 1989,) 47.

8 Ibid., 54.

9 Lee Kloepfer, *I Remember Ouray, Colorado 1927 to 1939*, (Lakewood: Copy Setters, 1984,) 50.

10 Hazel W. Dalziel, *Joyful Childhood Memories of a Pioneer Woman (Some Not So Joyful)*, (no city: Jack Dalziel and Kirby Dalziel Brock, 1988,) 30.

11 O. Ray Dodson, ed., *The Promised Land—Homestead Memories*, 139.

12 Lois Flansburg Haaglund, *Tough, Willing, and Able: Tales of a Montana Family*, (Missoula: Mountain Press Publishing Co., 1997,) 18.

13 Georgia Schad, *Mary E. Hatfield LaFollette: My Pioneer Mother*, (Weiser, Idaho: Commercial Printers & Publishers, 1954,) 118–19.

14 Elyse Deffke Bliss with Alice Cora Dickerson, *Apples of the Mummy's Eye: The Dickerson Sisters*, (Bellvue, Colorado: Elyse Deffke Bliss, 1994,) 21, 47.

15 Anonymous, 1907–8, unpublished journal, Sandra Dallas collection.

16 Julie Jones-Eddy, *Homesteading Women: An Oral History of Colorado, 1890–1950*, (New York: Twayne Publishers, 1992,) 10, 45, 151.

17 Sandra Dallas, interview with Ila Small Lingelbach, Brighton, Feb. 28, 2002.

18 Elyse Deffke Bliss with Alice Cora Dickerson, *Apples of the Mummy's Eye: The Dickerson Sisters*, 115.

19 Sandra Dallas, interview with Pat Hubbard, Denver, March 7, 2002.

20 Sandra Dallas, interview with Ila Small Lingelbach, Brighton, Feb. 28, 2002.

21 Sandra Dallas, interview with Margaret Geick, Denver, May 14, 2002.

22 Accession worksheet, Colorado Springs Pioneers Museum, Cat. No. A81-79-1.

23 Barbara Brackman, "Colorado Patterns," *Quilter's Newsletter Magazine*, Vol. 18, No. 2, Feb. 1987, (Wheatridge: Leman Publications Inc.,) 32–34.

24 William Rush Dunton, Jr., *Old Quilts*, (Catonsville: self-published, 1946,) 1, 4, 18.

25 Anonymous, "Quilting Bee," *Colorado Prospector*, Vol. 13, No. 6, June 1982, (Englewood: Colorado Prospector Inc.,) 4.

26 Hazel W. Dalziel, *Joyful Childhood Memories of a Pioneer Woman (Some Not So Joyful)*, 30–32.

27 Zoe Perrin and Frankie Wilson, "Mabel Ranson Gore," *Women As Tall As Our Mountain: Mini-biographies of Summit County Women*. (Summit County: Village Printer, 1976,) 40–42. Sandra Dallas, interview with Zoe Perrin, Denver, circa 1970.

28 Elyse Deffke Bliss with Alice Cora Dickerson, *Apples of the Mummy's Eye: The Dickerson Sisters*, 116.

29 Mary Knackstedt Dyck, *Waiting on the Bounty: The Dust Bowl Diary of Mary Knackstedt Dyck*, Pamela Riney-Kehrberg, ed. (Iowa City: University of Iowa Press, 1999,) 58, 61, 130, 134, 156, 173, 214, 285, 296, 309, 311.

30 Anonymous, "Little Locals," Colorado Prospector, Vol. 13, No. 6, June 1982, 4.

31 Sandra Dallas, interview with Jeananne Wright, Golden, Feb. 13, 2003.

32 Ibid.

33 Sandra Dallas, interview with Alberta Iliff Shattuck, Englewood, Jan. 21, 2002.

34 Anonymous, "The Way It Was Told," *Colorado Prospector*, Vol. 13, No. 6, June 1982, 2.

35 Harriett Mavity Dallas, unpublished journal, Sandra Dallas collection.

36 Sandra Dallas, interview with Ila Small Lingelbach, Brighton, Feb. 28, 2002.

37 Grace Snyder with Nellie Snyder Yost, *No Time On My Hands*, (Caldwell: Caxton Printers Ltd., 1963. Reprint: Lincoln: University of Nebraska Press, 1986,) 507, 518.

38 Nell Brown Propst, *Those Strenuous Dames of the Colorado Prairie*, (Boulder: Pruett Publishing Co., 1982,) 187–88.

39 Belle Turnbull, "Goose Pasture," *The Tenmile Range*, (Iowa City: Prairie Press, 1957,) 43.

40 Anne Ellis, *Life of an Ordinary Woman*, 241–42.

41 Carolyn O'Bagy Davis, *Quilted All Day: The Prairie Journals of Ida Chambers Melugin*, (Tucson: Sanpete Publications, 1993,) 64.

42 Anonymous, "The Way It Was Told," *Colorado Prospector*, Vol. 13, No. 6, June, 1982, 2.

43 Anonymous, "Navy Mothers requested to make Marine quilts," *Clear Creek Courant*, Vol. 29, No. 17, Sec. B, Dec. 5, 2001, (Idaho Springs: Clear Creek Publishing LLC,) 3.

44 "Commemorative World War II Quilt: Ida Johnson Beattie, 1942–45," 82.274.1, Colorado Historical Society.

45 Grace Snyder with Nellie Snyder Yost, *No Time On My Hands*, 454–55.

46 Sandra Dallas, telephone interview with Marie Overdier, March 12, 2003.

47 Anonymous, *Preserving Patterns: The Quilts of Charlott Jane Whitehill*, (Denver: Denver Art Museum, n.d.,) n.p.

48 Sandra Dallas interview with Jeananne Wright, Golden, Feb. 13, 2003.

49 Ruth E. Finley, *Old Patchwork Quilts And The Women Who Made Them*, (no city: Charles T. Branford Co., 1929,) 194–7.

50 Auriel Oram Sandstead, *A Cartouche Collection: Prairie-Patched Medallions: 20th Century Pictographs for Quilting from the Short Grass Prairie of Northeastern Colorado*, (Sterling: Signal Graphics Printing, n.d.,) 4–22. Sandra Dallas, telephone interview with Auriel Oram Sandstead, Jan. 28, 2003.

51 All Lula Evans information comes from unpublished information in the Colorado Springs Pioneers Museum.

Quilting Again

1 Sandra Dallas, interview with Cindy Harp, Littleton, May 28, 2003.

2 Sandra Dallas, telephone interview with Roberta Spillman, May 29, 2003.

3 Sandra Dallas, telephone interview with Opal Roderick, May 29, 2003.

4 Sandra D. Atchison, "Letter from Harveyville, Kansas: Something Made to Last," *Business Week*. (New York: McGraw-Hill Inc., May 11, 1992,) 28 A–D.

5 Jonathan Holstein, *American Pieced Quilts*, (New York: Viking Press, 1972,) 7.

6   Imelda G. DeGraw, *The Denver Art Museum Quilts and Coverlets*, (Denver: The Denver Art Museum, 1974,) n.p. Sandra Dallas telephone with Imelda DeGraw, June 7, 2003.

7   Nanette Simonds, interview with Shirley Sanden, Golden, Feb. 20, 2003.

8   Sandra Dallas, interview with Cindy Harp, Littleton, May 28, 2003.

9   Alfred Allan Lewis, *The Mountain Artisans Quilting Book*, (New York: Macmillan Publishing Co Inc., 1973,) 33, 68–9, 76, 115.

10   Sandra Dallas, telephone interview with Bonnie Leman, June 16, 2003.

11   Anonymous, *Women's Gold*, (Denver: no publisher, 1977,) 2–4, 20–22. Sandra Dallas, interview with Connie Primus, Georgetown, May 25, 2003. Sandra Dallas, interview with Libbie Gottschalk, Denver, May 29, 2003.

12   Opal Frey notes, June, 2003.

13   Sandra D. Atchison, "Letter from Harveyville, Kansas: Something Made to Last," *Business Week*, May 11, 1992, 28 D.

14   Nanette Simonds, interview with Shirley Sanden, Golden, Feb. 18, 2003, and with Kaila Mills, Fraser, May 4, 2003.

15   Sandra Dallas, telephone interview with Bonnie Leman, June 16, 2003.

16   Sandra Dallas, interview with Marge Hedges, Georgetown, May 24, 2003.

17   Ibid.

18   Sandra Dallas, interview with Opal Frey, Golden, June 6, 2003.

19   Sandra Dallas, interview with Janet Finley, Golden, June 6, 2003.

20   Sandra Dallas, interview with Marge Hedges, Georgetown, May 24, 2003.

21   Sandra Dallas, interview with Ricky Tims, Arvada, June 10, 2003.

22   Sandra Dallas, telephone interview with David Taylor, June 8, 2003.

23   Libbie Gottschalk, "History of the Label Quilt," unpublished manuscript (Littleton: Libbie Gottschalk collection,) 2003.

24   Sandra Dallas, interview with Pat Hubbard, Denver, March 7, 2002.

25   Sandra Dallas, interview with Patty Hawkins, Estes Park, June 23, 2003.

26   Sandra Dallas, interview with Judith Trager, Boulder, May 27, 2003.

27   Sandra Dallas, interview with Patty Hawkins, June 23, 2003.

28   Sandra Dallas, interview with Marge Hedges, Georgetown, May 24, 2003.

29   Bonnie McFadden letter, Feb. 20, 2003.

30   Sandra Dallas, interview with Ricky Tims, Arvada, June 10, 2003.

Binding Off

1   Sandra Dallas, interview with Jeananne Wright, Golden, Feb. 13, 2003, and subsequent interviews.

2   Sandra Dallas, telephone interview with Mary Ann Schmidt, Feb. 12, 2003.

3   Sandra Dallas, telephone interview with Barbara Brackman, Feb. 15, 2003.

4   Sandra Dallas, interview with Jeananne Wright, Golden, Feb. 13, 2003.

5   Sandra Dallas, interview with Alisa Zahller, Denver, Jan., 2002.

6   Sandra Dallas, interview with Jeananne Wright, Golden, Feb. 13, 2003.

7   All Eugenia Mitchell quotes come from Barbara Daubenspeck interviews with Eugenia Mitchell, Golden, 1990–1993.

8   Sandra Dallas, telephone interview with Mary Ellen Gray, April 7, 2003.

9   Sandra Dallas, telephone interview with Teri DuBois, March 14, 2003.

10   Sandra Dallas, telephone interview with Mary Ann Schmidt, Feb. 12, 2003.

11   Sandra Dallas, telephone interview with Marie Overdier, March 12, 2003.

12   Sandra Dallas, telephone interview with Mary Ann Schmidt, Feb. 12, 2003.

13   Sandra Dallas, telephone interview with Mary Ellen Gray, April 7, 2003.

Bibliography

Books

A Hand Book to the Gold Fields of Nebraska and Kansas. Chicago: D.B. Cooke & Co., 1859.

Adams, Ramon F. Cowboy Lingo: A Dictionary of the Slack-Jaw Words and Whangdoodle Ways of the American West. Boston: Houghton Mifflin Co., 1936.

———. Western Words: A Dictionary of the American West. Norman: University of Oklahoma Press, 1968.

Aldrich, Bess Streeter. The Rim of the Prairie. Lincoln: University of Nebraska Press, 1966.

Bancroft, Caroline. Augusta Tabor: Her Side of the Scandal. Boulder: Johnson Publishing Co., 1961.

———. Silver Queen: The Fabulous Story of Baby Doe Tabor. Boulder: Johnson Publishing Co., 1965.

Barns, Cass G. The Sod House. Lincoln: University of Nebraska Press, 1970.

Beard, Carrie Hunt. Colorado Gold Rush Days: Memories of a Childhood in the Eighties and Nineties. New York: Exposition Press, 1964.

Blevins, Winfred. Dictionary of the American West. New York: Facts On File, 1993.

Bliss, Elyse Deffke, with Alice C. Dickerson. Apples of the Mummy's Eye: The Dickerson Sisters. Bellvue, Colorado: Elise Deffke Bliss, 1994.

Brackman, Barbara, Jennie A. Chinn, Gayle R. Davis, Terry Thompson, Sara Reimer Farley and Nancy Hornback. Kansas Quilts & Quilters. Lawrence: University Press of Kansas, 1993.

Brandon, Ruth. A Capitalist Romance: Singer and the Sewing Machine. Philadelphia: J.B. Lippincott Co., 1977.

Brown, Georgina. The Shining Mountains. Gunnison: B&B Printers, 1976.

Butruille, Susan G. Women's Voices from the Oregon Trail. Boise: Tamarack Books Inc., 1993.

———. Women's Voices from the Western Frontier. Boise: Tamarack Books Inc., 1995.

Chase, A.W. Dr. Chase's Recipes; or, Information for Everybody: An Invaluable Collection of About Eight Hundred Practical Recipes. Ann Arbor: A.W. Chase, 1865.

Child, L. Maria. The American Frugal Housewife. New York: Samuel S. & William Wood, 1838.

———. The Girl's Own Book. New York: Clark Austin & Co., 1833. Reprint, Chester, Conn.: Applewood Books, n.d.

Cleaveland, Agnes Morley. No Life for a Lady. Boston: Houghton Mifflin Co., 1941. Reprint, Lincoln: University of Nebraska Press, 1977.

Cooke, Lucy Rutledge. Crossing the Plains In 1852: Narrative of a Trip from Iowa to "The Land of Gold," As Told in Letters Written During the Journey. Fairfield, Wash.: Ye Galleon Press, n.d.

Covington, Kae. Gathered in Time: Utah Quilts and Their Makers, Settlement to 1950. Salt Lake City: University of Utah Press, 1997.

Crews, Patricia Cox, and Ronald C. Naugle, eds. Nebraska Quilts & Quiltmakers. Lincoln: University of Nebraska Press, 1991.

Cross, Mary Bywater. Quilts and Women of the Mormon Migrations: Treasures of Transition. Nashville: Rutledge Hill Press, 1996.

———. Treasures in the Trunk: Quilts of the Oregon Trail. Nashville: Rutledge Hill Press, 1993.

Dallas, Sandra. Gold and Gothic. Denver: Lick Skillet Press, 1967.

Dalziel, Hazel W. Joyful Childhood Memories of a Pioneer Woman (Some Not So Joyful). Lakewood: Jack Dalziel and Kirby Dalziel Brock, 1988.

Davis, Carolyn O'Bagy. Quilted All Day: The Prairie Journals of Ida Chambers Melugin. Tucson: Sanpete Publications, 1993.

DeGraw, Imelda G. Quilts and Coverlets. Denver: Denver Art Museum, 1974.

Denney, Hazel. Veteran, District 13: Homesteading in Goshen Hole. Philadelphia: Dorrance & Co., 1976.

Dodson, O. Ray. The Promised Land Homestead Memories. Pueblo: Prairie Heritage Press, 1989.

Dunton, William Rush, Jr. Old Quilts. Catonsville, Md.: William Rush Dunton Jr., 1946.

Ellis, Anne. Plain Anne Ellis: More About the Life of an Ordinary Woman. Boston: Houghton Mifflin Co., 1931. Reprint, Lincoln: University of Nebraska Press, 1984.

———. The Life of an Ordinary Woman. Boston: Houghton Mifflin Co., 1929.

Fanning, Mary. For the Golden Times. Denver: John Waddell Press, 1977.

Faragher, John Mack. Women and Men on the Overland Trail. New Haven: Yale University Press, 1979.

Ferril, Thomas Hornsby. Westering. New Haven: Yale University Press, 1934.

Fink, Deborah. Agrarian Women: Wives and Mothers in Rural Nebraska, 1880–1940. Chapel Hill: University of North Carolina Press, 1992.

Finley, Ruth E. *Old Patchwork Quilts and the Women Who Made Them*. No city: Charles T. Branford Co., 1980.

Fischer, Christiane, ed. *Let Them Speak for Themselves: Women in the American West 1849–1900*. Hamden: Archon Books, 1977.

Foote, Mary Hallock. *A Victorian Gentlewoman in the Far West: The Reminiscences of Mary Hallock Foote*. San Marino: Huntington Library, 1980.

Freeman, Roland L. *A Communion of the Spirits: African-American Quilters, Preservers, and Their Stories*. Nashville: Rutledge Hill Press, 1996.

French, Emily. *Emily: The Diary of a Hard-Worked Woman*. Lincoln: University of Nebraska Press, 1987.

George, Gerald and Cindy Sherrell-Leo. *Starting Right: A Basic Guide to Museum Planning*. Nashville: American Association for State and Local History, 1986.

Gibbens, Byrd, ed. *This Is a Strange Country: Letters of a Westering Family, 1880–1906*. Albuquerque: University of New Mexico Press, 1988.

Greenwood, Annie Pike. *We Sagebrush Folks*. Moscow: University of Idaho Press, 1988.

Haaglund, Lois Flansburg. *Tough, Willing, and Able: Tales of a Montana Family*. Missoula: Mountain Press Publishing Co., 1997.

Hale, Sarah Jane, ed. *Good Little Girls' Book*. New York: McLoughlin Bros., n.d.

Hill, Alice Polk. *Tales of the Colorado Pioneers*. Denver: Pierson & Gardner, 1884. Reprint, Glorieta: Rio Grande Press Inc., 1976.

Holmes, Kenneth L., and David C. Duniway, eds. *Covered Wagon Women: Diaries & Letters from the Western Trails 1840–1890*, 11 vols. Glendale: Arthur H. Clark, 1983–93.

Holstein, Jonathan. *American Pieced Quilts*. New York: Viking Press, 1972.

Houck, Carter. *The Quilt Encyclopedia Illustrated*. New York: Harry N. Abrams, Inc., 1991.

Ise, John. *Sod and Stubble*. Lincoln: University of Nebraska Press, 1967.

Jeffrey, Julie Roy. *Frontier Women*. New York: Hill and Wang, 1998.

——— . *Frontier Women: The Trans-Mississippi West 1840–1880*. New York: Hill and Wang, 1979.

Jones-Eddy, Julie. *Homesteading Women: An Oral History of Colorado 1890–1950*. New York: Twayne Publishers, 1992.

Kiracofe, Roderick. *The American Quilt: A History of Cloth and Comfort 1750–1950*. New York: Clarkson Potter Publishers, 1993.

Kloepfer, Lee. *I Remember Ouray, Colorado 1927–1939*. Lakewood: Copy Setters, 1984.

Laury, Jean Ray. *Ho for California! Pioneer Women and Their Quilts*. New York: E.P. Dutton, 1990.

Leckie, Shirley Anne. *The Colonel's Lady on the Western Frontier: The Correspondence of Alice Kirk Grierson*. Lincoln: University of Nebraska Press, 1989.

Lewis, Alfred Allan. *The Mountain Artisans Quilting Book*. New York: Macmillan Publishing Co. Inc., 1973.

Lockley, Fred. *Conversations with Pioneer Women*. Eugene: Rainy Day Press, 1981.

Luchetti, Cathy. *Women of the West*. St. George, Utah: Antelope Island Press, 1982.

Mattes, Merrill J. *The Great Platte River Road*. Lincoln: Nebraska State Historical Society, 1969.

Maxwell, William Audley. *Crossing the Plains Days of '57: A Narrative of Early Emigrant Travel to California by the Ox-Team Method*. San Francisco: Sunset Publishing House, 1915.

McLean, Evalyn Walsh. *Father Struck It Rich*. Boston: Little, Brown, and Co., 1936.

McNitt, Orpha Baldwin and Alice McNitt Montgomery. *Letters from a Frontier Bride, Prairie Christmas and Other Stories*. No city: No publisher, 1993.

Miller, Darlis A. *Mary Hallock Foote: Author-Illustrator of the American West*. Norman: University of Oklahoma Press, 2002.

Miller, Michala. *The View from the Folding Chairs*. Montrose, Colorado: Western Reflections Publishing Co., 2001.

Morgan, Dale, ed. *Overland in 1846: Diaries and Letters of the California-Oregon Trail*, vols. 1–2. Georgetown, Calif.: Talisman Press, 1963.

Moynihan, Ruth B., Susan Armitage, and Christine Fischer Dichamp. *So Much to Be Done: Women Settlers on the Mining and Ranching Frontier*. Lincoln: University of Nebraska Press, 1990.

Myres, Sandra L., ed. *Ho for California! Women's Overland Diaries from the Huntington Library*. San Marino: Huntington Library, 1980.

——— . *Westering Women and the Frontier Experience 1800–1915*. Albuquerque: University of New Mexico Press, 1982.

Orlofsky, Patsy and Myron, *Quilts in America*. New York: McGraw-Hill Book Co., 1974.

Paden, Irene D. *The Wake of the Prairie Schooner*. Gerald, Mo.: Patrice Press, 1985.

Peavy, Linda and Ursula Smith. *Pioneer Women: The Lives of Women on the Frontier*. New York: Smithmark Publishers, 1996.

——— . *The Gold Rush Widows of Little Falls: A Story Drawn from the Letters of Pamelia and James Fergus*. St. Paul: Minnesota Historical Society Press, 1990.

——— . *Women in Waiting in the Westward Movement: Life on the Home Frontier*. Norman: University of Oklahoma Press, 1994.

Peto, Florence. *Historic Quilts*. New York: American Historical Co. Inc., 1939.

——— . *Quilts and Coverlets: A History of a Charming Native Art Together with a Manuel of Instructions for Beginners*. New York: Chanticleer Press, 1949.

Pratt, ? and ? Hunt. *Guide to the Gold Mines of Kansas*. Chicago: Pratt & Hunt, 1859.

Propst, Nell Brown. *Those Strenuous Dames of the Colorado Prairie*. Boulder: Pruett Publishing Co., 1982.

Redpath, James and Richard J. Hinton. *Hand-Book to Kansas Territory and the Rocky Mountains' Gold Region*. New York: J.H. Colton, 1859.

Reed, ? *Reed's Guide to the Kansas Gold Region*. New York: J.H. Colton, 1859.

Reid, Agnes Just. *Letters of Long Ago*. Salt Lake City: University of Utah Library, 1973.

Riley, Glenda. *The Female Frontier: A Comparative View of Women on the Prairie and the Plains*. Lawrence: University Press of Kansas, 1988.

——— . *Women and Indians on the Frontier, 1825–1915*. Albuquerque: University of New Mexico Press, 1984.

Riney-Kehrberg, Pamela. *Waiting on the Bounty: The Dust Bowl Diary of Mary Knackstedt Dyck*. Iowa City: University of Iowa Press, 1999.

Robertson, Elizabeth Wells. *American Quilts*. New York: Studio Publications Inc., 1948.

Rogers, Maria M. *In Other Words: Oral Histories of the Colorado Frontier*. Golden: Fulcrum Publishing, 1995.

Ross, Nancy Wilson. *Westward the Women*. San Francisco: North Point Press, 1985.

Safford, Carleton L., and Robert Bishop. *America's Quilts and Coverlets*. New York: E.P. Dutton & Co. Inc., 1972.

Sandstead, Auriel Oram. *A Cartouche Collection: Prairie-Patched Medallions: 20th Century Pictographs for Quilting from the Short Grass Prairie of Northeastern Colorado*, 2 vols. Sterling, Colorado: Signal Graphics Printing, n.d.

Sanford, Mollie Dorsey. *Mollie: The Journal of Mollie Dorsey Sanford in Nebraska and Colorado Territories, 1857–1866*. Lincoln: University of Nebraska Press, 1976.

Sanger, William W. *The History of Prostitution: Its Extent, Causes and Effects Throughout the World*. New York: Eugenics Publishing Co., 1939. Reprint, New York: AMS Press Inc., 1974.

Schad, Georgia. *Mary E. Hatfield LaFollette: My Pioneer Mother*. Weiser, Idaho: Commercial Printers & Publishers, 1954.

Schlissel, Lillian. *Women's Diaries of the Westward Journey*. New York: Schocken Books, 1982.

Secrest, Clark. *Hell's Belles: Denver's Brides of the Multitudes*. Aurora: Hindsight Historical Publications, 1996.

Smith, Eugene. *Pioneer Epic*. Boulder: Johnson Publishing Co., 1951.

Snyder, Grace and Nellie Snyder Yost. *No Time on My Hands*. Lincoln: University of Nebraska Press, 1986.

Spring, Agnes Wright, ed. *A Bloomer Girl on Pike's Peak, 1858*. Denver: Denver Public Library, 1949.

Springer, Marlene and Haskell Springer, eds. *Plains Woman: The Diary of Martha Farnsworth, 1882–1922*. Bloomington: Indiana University Press, 1988.

Steadfast in Faith: A Book of Memories. 1874–1999. Georgetown, Colorado: First United Presbyterian Church, 1999.

Steward, Elinore Pruitt. *Letters of a Woman Homesteader*. Lincoln: University of Nebraska Press, 1961.

Stratton, Joanna L. *Pioneer Women: Voices from the Kansas Frontier*. New York: Simon and Schuster, 1981.

Thane, James L. Jr., ed. *A Governor's Wife on the Mining Frontier: The Letters of Mary Edgerton from Montana, 1863–1865*. Salt Lake City: University of Utah Library, 1976.

Turnbull, Belle. *Goldboat*. Boston: Houghton Mifflin Co., 1940.

———. *The Far Side of the Hill*. New York: Crown Publishers Inc., 1953.

———. *The Tenmile Range*. Iowa City: Prairie Press, 1957.

Unruh, John D. Jr. *The Plains Across: The Overland Emigrants and the Trans-Mississippi West, 1840–60*. Urbana: University of Illinois Press, 1979.

Volunteers of the State Historical Society of Colorado. *Pioneer Potluck: Stories and Recipes of Early Colorado*. Denver: State Historical Society of Colorado, 1963.

Wagenbach, Lorraine, and Jo Ann E. Thistlewood. *Golden: The 19th Century: A Colorado Chronicle*. Littleton: Harbinger House, 1987.

Warren, Elizabeth V., and Sharon L. Eisenstat. *Glorious American Quilts: The Quilt Collection of the Museum of American Folk Art*. New York: Penguin Studio, 1996.

Watson, Jeanne Hamilton, ed. *To the Land of Gold and Wickedness: The 1848–59 Diary of Lorena L. Hays*. St. Louis: Patrice Press, 1988.

Webber, Bert, ed. *The Oregon & California Trail Diary of Jane Gould in 1862*. Medford: Webb Research Group, 1993.

Webster, Marie D. *Quilts: Their Story and How to Make Them*. Marion, Indiana: Marie D. Webster, 1929.

Women As Tall As Our Mountains: Mini-biographies of Summit County Women. Summit County: PEO Chapter FU, n.d.

Women's Gold. Denver: No publisher, 1977.

Zopf, Dorothy R. *Surviving the Winter: The Evolution of Quiltmaking in New Mexico*. Albuquerque: University of New Mexico Press, 2001.

Articles

Atchison, Sandra D. "Letter from Harveyville, Kansas: Something Made to Last." *Business Week*. New York: McGraw-Hill Inc., May 11, 1992.

Brackman, Barbara. "Applications and Innovations: Three Decades of Revivals, Trends, and Revolutions." *Quilter's Newsletter Magazine*. Wheat Ridge, Colo.: Leman Publications Inc., Sept., 1999.

———. "Colorado Patterns." *Quilter's Newsletter Magazine*. Wheat Ridge, Colo.: Leman Publications Inc., Feb., 1987.

———. "Memories: Looking Back at Five Years of Quilting Events." *Quilter's Newsletter Magazine*. Wheat Ridge, Colo.: Leman Publications Inc., Sept., 1989.

Leman, Bonnie and Marie Shirer. "A Quilting Survey: Where We've Been, Where We Are, and Where We're Going." *Quilter's Newsletter Magazine*, 15th Anniversary Issue. Wheat Ridge: Leman Publication Inc., 1984.

Malcolm, Janet. "On and Off the Avenue." *The New Yorker*. New York: Condé Nast Publications, Sept. 4, 1971.

Spears, Jeannie M. "Keepers of the Flame: Quilters' Stories from the '40s, '50s and '60s." *Quilter's Newsletter Magazine*. Wheat Ridge: Leman Publications Inc., Sept. 1999, April 2000.

Townsend, Louise O. "What Was New and News in Quilting." *Quilter's Newsletter Magazine*, 15th Anniversary Issue. Wheat Ridge: Leman Publications Inc., 1984.

Witter, Mrs. Daniel. "Pioneer Life." *The Colorado Magazine*. Denver: The State Historical and Natural History Society of Colorado, Dec. 1927.

Unpublished Journals and Manuscripts

Anonymous Engagements Memorandum Book, 1907. Denver: Sandra Dallas collection.

Anonymous journal, 1883. Sandra Dallas collection.

Jessie Babcock journal. Littleton: Littleton Historical Museum.

Harriett Mavity Dallas journal, 1931–35. Sandra Dallas collection.

Hazel Green journal, 1884–85. Sandra Dallas collection

Nellie Jean Nichols journal. Colorado Historical Society.

Mollie Sanford Dorsey journal, "The Old Ranch Near Littleton, Colorado: Diary of Mollie Dorsey Sanford, May 2, 1895–March 19, 1900." Littleton. Littleton Historical Museum.

Publications

Clear Creek Courant

Denver Post

Colorado Prospector

Golden Globe

Kansas History: A Journal of the Central Plains

Quilter's Newsletter Magazine

Rocky Mountain News

The Golden Transcript

Credits

All color photographs of quilts are by Povy Kendal Atchison and are reproduced courtesy of The Rocky Mountain Quilt Museum, Golden, Colorado, unless otherwise noted. All uncredited vintage photographs are in a private collection.

i. Courtesy of Colorado Historical Society.

iii. Photograph by Povy Kendal Atchison, courtesy of Sandra Dallas.

viii. Photograph by Povy Kendal Atchison at Boreas Pass, near Breckenridge.

6. Photograph by Povy Kendal Atchison at Clear Creek History Park, Golden.

10. Courtesy of State Historical Society of Iowa.

18. Courtesy of Denver Public Library, Western History Department.

28. Photograph by Povy Kendal Atchison at Clear Creek History Park, Golden.

32. Courtesy of Denver Public Library, Western History Department.

51. Courtesy of Denver Public Library, Western History Department.

52. Courtesy of Colorado Historical Society.

60. Photograph by Povy Kendal Atchison in Golden.

64. (Top), courtesy of Cindy Brick.

67. Courtesy of Denver Public Library, Western History Department.

68. Courtesy of Colorado Springs Pioneers Museum.

72. Courtesy of Denver Public Library, Western History Department.

74. Courtesy of Loyd Files Research Library, Museum of Western Colorado.

77. Courtesy of Colorado Historical Society.

78. Photograph by Sandra Dallas. Courtesy of Denver Public Library, Western History Department.

81. Courtesy of Ron Penton.

82. Photograph by Ford Optical Co. Courtesy of Denver Public Library, Western History Department.

90. Photograph by Povy Kendal Atchison.

91. Photograph by Povy Kendal Atchison.

92. Courtesy of Auriel Oram Sandstead.

94. Courtesy of Colorado Springs Pioneers Museum.

95. Courtesy of Colorado Springs Pioneers Museum.

96. Photograph by Povy Kendal Atchison at Red Rocks.

103. Courtesy of Denver Art Museum.

105. Courtesy of Libbie Gottschalk.

109. Courtesy of Montana Historical Society, Helena.

110. (Bottom), courtesy of Carol Goin.

112. Courtesy of Ricky Tims.

115. Photograph by Povy Kendal Atchison.

118. Photograph by Povy Kendal Atchison.

119. Courtesy of Mary Ann Schmidt.

121. Photograph by Povy Kendal Atchison.

122. Photographs by Povy Kendal Atchison.

123. Courtesy of Mary Ann Schmidt.

124. Photograph by Povy Kendal Atchison at Boreas Pass, near Breckenridge.

127. Photograph by Povy Kendal Atchison.

132. Courtesy of Ruben Hartmeister.

136. (Bottom), courtesy of Rocky Mountain Quilt Museum.

140. Photograph by Povy Kendal Atchison.

Index